"I know Kim King personally and can testify that she takes the challenge in 1 Timothy 6:17-19 to live generously seriously. In this timely book, she encourages you to do the same while showing you how. You will not regret applying her sage advice."
Russ Crosson, president and CEO, Ronald Blue & Co.

"We do not typically think about giving as an adventure, but *When Women Give* opens our hearts and minds to the joy of living generously. Too often we sit in the pews and hear about giving to meet a church budget or to build a new church facility. We miss the connection of partnering with God to let him direct how he wants us to use his money and resources. *When Women Give* shares inspiring stories of generous giving but also provides practical information and tools for us to use in joining God on the journey of generosity."
Laurie Rachford, general counsel, ExxonMobil Chemical Company

"I first met Kim ten years ago. Her journey of growing generosity has been a great encouragement to me and all those who know her. In her new book, she offers useful insights and practical steps for anyone thinking about questions related to money and giving. I wholeheartedly recommend *When Women Give*. Kim is another example of the reality that there are no unhappy generous people!"
Todd Harper, president, Generous Giving

"*When Women Give* clarifies the impact of my role as a professional and paints an very clear picture of the impact of my financial contributions—a picture I could only see before in black and white. The final chapter pierced my heart, leaving it as fertile soil ready to receive God's best, to give my firstfruits and storm my office Monday morning with reckless abandon. I will conquer my market share and live the great adventure! What if women really grabbed ahold of this concept? Imagine the advancement of God's kingdom here on earth."
Brandi McDonald, executive managing director, Newmark Grubb Knight Frank

"I was captivated by the stories shared in Kim King's book. As I work with women in the workplace, I'm surprised at the lack of understanding of financial tools available to enable giving in a much bigger way than most imagine. Not only does Kim provide 'giving' guidance, but she shares stories where God truly takes hearts and opens them to never-thought-about possibilities regarding generosity."
Diane Paddison, founder of 4word, author of *Work, Love, Pray,* former global executive team of two Fortune 500 companies and one Fortune 1000 company

"Inspiration, education, and practical roadmap all in one. As if that weren't enough, the laugh-out-loud moments are pure delight. A helpful read for anyone curious about generosity and the world of nonprofits."

Sandy Swider, leadership coach, managing director of local groups, 4word Women

"Kim King has written an outstanding book on generosity—a topic that is embodied with integrity in her daily life. This is not just a book for women, but one that men and women alike should read. It's compelling, comprehensive, and filled with biblical and practical wisdom. It's well researched and full of personal stories and practical tools. I commend it to you highly."

Jim Herrington, cofounder, Faithwalking

"Several things have struck me since I first met Kim King a decade and a half ago: she has a positive and generous spirit, she is a serious follower of Jesus, and she is a passionate and effective teacher. Kim approaches this subject matter with much the same curiosity, openness, and intentionality. She studied financial generosity, opened herself up to the prompting of the Spirit, and then experimented—courageously expanding its hold on her life. With her storytelling and insights, Kim found a way to draw me and others in. This is Kim's big idea in her own words: 'The greater the giving, the greater the adventure, and the greater the adventure, the greater the joy.' As Gary Haugen, founder and director of International Justice Mission says, 'Joy is the fuel for the passion of our obedience.' This could be the subtitle for the book. As a Christian man having grown up in the generation that saw an avalanche of cultural change with women entering the workforce outside the home, I'm fascinated with not only the statistics Kim reports, but the stories that bring these statistics to life. This is must-read for women who want to understand (and be empowered by understanding) gender differences and similarities around giving, generosity, and philanthropy, but also for men who want to nurture these things—and sometimes get out of the way."

John Montgomery, chairman and chief investment officer, Bridgeway Capital Management

"When God blesses us with the talent and opportunity that enables us to achieve financial success, we want to honor him. But we need a game plan. This book provides an eye-opening common-sense approach for every woman seeking a life of kingdom giving and living. Whether serving on a board or providing financial support, you will learn much and find yourself well equipped to fulfill God's plan for his kingdom."

Fran McKinney, senior VP, McGriff, Seibels & Williams

When Women Give

THE ADVENTURE OF A GENEROUS LIFE

KIM KING

Foreword by PETER GREER

IVP Books
An imprint of InterVarsity Press
Downers Grove, Illinois

InterVarsity Press

P.O. Box 1400, Downers Grove, IL 60515-1426

ivpress.com

email@ivpress.com

InterVarsity Press® is the book-publishing division of InterVarsity Christian Fellowship/USA®, a movement of students and faculty active on campus at hundreds of universities, colleges, and schools of nursing in the United States of America, and a member movement of the International Fellowship of Evangelical Students. For information about local and regional activities, visit intervarsity.org.

All Scripture quotations, unless otherwise indicated, are taken from THE HOLY BIBLE, NEW INTERNATIONAL VERSION®, NIV® Copyright © 1973, 1978, 1984, 2011 by Biblica, Inc.™ Used by permission. All rights reserved worldwide.

While any stories in this book are true, some names and identifying information may have been changed to protect the privacy of individuals.

Cover design: Cindy Kiple

Interior design: Jeanna Wiggins

Images: fountain pen: © Azure-Dragon/iStockphoto
golden bracelet: © Cristiano Almeida/EyeEm/Getty Images

ISBN 978-0-8308-4511-8 (print)

ISBN 978-0-8308-9089-7 (digital)

Printed in the United States of America ♾

Library of Congress Cataloging-in-Publication Data

Names: King, Kim, 1957- author.

Title: When women give : the adventure of a generous life / Kim King ; foreword by Peter Greer.

Description: Downers Grove : InterVarsity Press, 2017. | Includes bibliographical references.

Identifiers: LCCN 2017019255 (print) | LCCN 2017024189 (ebook) | ISBN 9780830890897 (eBook) | ISBN 9780830845118 (pbk. : alk. paper)

Subjects: LCSH: Christian women--Religious life. | Christian giving. | Generosity--Religious aspects--Christianity. | Humanitarianism--Religious aspects--Christianity.

Classification: LCC BV4527 (ebook) | LCC BV4527 .K47495 2017 (print) | DDC 248/.6082--dc23

LC record available at https://lccn.loc.gov/2017019255

| P | 25 | 24 | 23 | 22 | 21 | 20 | 19 | 18 | 17 | 16 | 15 | 14 | 13 | 12 | 11 | 10 | 9 | 8 | 7 | 6 | 5 | 4 | 3 | 2 | 1 |
| Y | 36 | 35 | 34 | 33 | 32 | 31 | 30 | 29 | 28 | 27 | 26 | 25 | 24 | 23 | 22 | 21 | 20 | 19 | 18 | 17 |

Contents

Part 4: Companions on the Journey

Part 5: The Adventure of Giving

Foreword

Peter Greer, President of HOPE International

Women are courageously generous.

Research conducted by the Women's Philanthropy Institute (WPI) in 2010 revealed that despite the fact that the income of women in the United States remains lower, their retirement savings are less, and their life expectancy is longer than men's across income levels, they give more to philanthropic causes than their male counterparts.[1] "In other words," as a 2016 *Wall Street Journal* article put it, "even though women tend to have fewer available resources as they age, they are giving larger portions of their wealth to charity than men."[2] Further, the WPI study shows that "American households headed by single females give 57% more than those headed by single males."[3]

At the same time, economic and social landscapes are shifting. More women are entering the workforce, and gender-based stereotypes about the role of women in financial decisions within their homes have been dismantled. Nancy Heiser, vice president of wealth management at UBS, observes, "Women are living longer, making more money and may be inheriting twice—once from their parents and again if they outlive their spouses."[4]

In short, women today have more access to and influence over wealth than any of their sisters before them. And the data tells us that they tend to use their resources in exceedingly generous ways.

There is nothing less than a revolution taking place. Already, gifts channeled by women toward philanthropic causes are making significant national and global impact—which will only increase in the years to come.

When Women Give explores these extraordinary trends, bringing to light not only the research behind the movement but also the powerful stories inspiring it. Whatever their context—from company leaders and community volunteers to mothers and entrepreneurs—women are exercising courageous generosity.

As an author, Kim hasn't simply written about the experience of others; she has lived out her own story of courageous generosity. Over the past decade, I've had the incredible privilege of watching Kim's journey, initially as a supporter of HOPE International, then as a board member, and now as a friend. Faithfully following God's leading, she has grasped the blessing and responsibility that comes with money.

Although this is a book written for women by a leading female philanthropist, the principles and stories within are for all people who want to live and serve with radical generosity. *When Women Give* will help you to discover the passions God has given you, inviting you to use them as a guide to direct your giving. It also extends the radical challenge to view your money as a God-given tool to be used to expand his kingdom around the world. What you discover within these pages will cause you to think deeply about the way you steward your resources—and your life.

While other writings about philanthropy lay out reasons *to* give, this book takes an unflinching look at the excuses we so often make for *not* giving. The stories in *When Women Give* fundamentally challenge the ways we stifle our generosity.

Ultimately, *When Women Give* serves as a call to move beyond our fears—that we don't have enough, that our giving can't make a difference, that by serving others we'll damage ourselves—so we can embark on the great adventure of a generous life.

At the heart of this book lies an invitation: be brave, step out, and watch how God provides.

PART 1

An Invitation to Give

CHAPTER 1

The Impact of One Woman

"What are we going to do?" asked Rachel.

For years, Rachel Gallagher and her husband, David, had operated Open Arms International, a ministry near Eldoret, Kenya.[1] Led by a board of Kenyans and others, Open Arms had a mission to rescue abandoned children in the area. The Gallaghers had created the Open Arms Village, where homes are built to house Christian Kenyan couples and their children—along with a number of abandoned children who live together as a family unit. The Open Arms Village includes these homes as well as school buildings, gardens, a dairy, and a medical clinic.

Rachel and David received news that a couple who had been donors for years couldn't give as they had in the past. Because this couple's contributions covered a major portion of the operation expenses, Rachel and David had to cut all but necessities.

As Open Arms' bank account shrank, the Gallaghers, families in the Village, and staff prayed and waited. They soon had to determine whether to cut staff and halt the building of much-needed new houses for children. During this time, Rachel said, "I'm not sure which will be more painful: letting go of faithful staff or turning away children needing a home."

Then an unexpected email arrived with news of a new donor. David and Rachel were shocked, and they humbly and joyfully thanked God. The donation would allow them to meet their current needs as they sought additional sources of funding.

When they shared the news with the staff in the Village, dancing and singing broke out as they praised God for his provision. They called the board of directors to share the good news.

The next day, David and Rachel experienced disappointment as great as their previous day's joy when they learned the new donor had made a mistake; the intent had been to give a considerably smaller gift. The difference between a comma and a decimal meant two fewer zeros. Their exhilaration disappeared like air out of a balloon.

David sent an email from Kenya to the donor, insisting on returning the gift. As he wrote the email, he thought to himself, "The Lord gives, and the Lord takes away. Wow, he gave and took away really fast on that one!"

Shortly after suffering that disappointment, they learned the donor was taking time to pray about whether to take funds back. David and Rachel didn't pray that the donor wouldn't ask for it back; they simply asked the Holy Spirit to guide.

The donor decided to give the full amount. David said, "We were jubilant when we learned the donor felt led to leave the donation in place. The donor shared that God was teaching her to live generously."

Rachel added, "I wasn't surprised when I learned that the donor was a woman. My experience is that women are often the heart behind a gift."

Women have so much to offer a world in need. They give their time, their abilities, and their resources.

Giving Time with Financial Sacrifice: Erica

Erica, an energetic young teacher, enjoyed her work at a charter school for children from low-income families. She attended an information session on human trafficking at her church in Houston and was shocked to hear that human trafficking is more prevalent today than at any other time in history. Most victims are women and children.

Outraged, Erica thought, *Someone should do something.* Then she heard God speak to her heart: "You should do something."

Houston is the largest city on Interstate 10 from Santa Monica, California, to Jacksonville, Florida—a corridor through which one in five individuals trafficked in the United States is transported. For this reason, Houston is a center for human trafficking. The victims are principally from Latin America, Africa, and Asia, as well as the United States.

"I had no idea that something so horrible existed in this world, let alone in the city I lived in," Erica said.

Because Houston is a major hub of human trafficking in the United States,[2] it's home to a number of organizations fighting human trafficking and caring for victims. Erica began serving with several Christian antitrafficking organizations and grew in her understanding of the complexity of the problem. While supporting their efforts financially, she also gave her time to help train volunteers to care for victims.

With a sad look, Erica said, "You would not believe what these victims have been through."

A number of groups in Houston are focused on trafficking, but Erica soon learned that coordination and sharing best practices was limited in the face of numerous challenges to fighting trafficking on a large scale. In addition, the organizations sometimes had different views on issues and practices. These challenges led to missed opportunities and limits in effectiveness. Erica saw improving coordination and communication as a great need, one she would pursue.

For more than a year, the idea of a place for connection, collaboration, and education remained on her heart. Her vision of such a place continued to grow, leading to plans for A 2nd Cup, a coffeehouse in Houston that would serve in the fight against human trafficking.

Action followed Erica's planning as A 2nd Cup collaborated with seven organizations and six churches. She leased a two-thousand-square-foot facility that will serve as the coffeehouse and contain multipurpose rooms for organizations to meet to work together. A 2nd Cup will also provide information on human trafficking to those who come just for a good cup of coffee. Lastly, the facility will serve as a place where victim-care organizations can provide counseling and education to victims.

With a growing passion for this mission, Erica faced a difficult decision: give up her regular job—and a dependable teacher's salary—to focus full-time on leading this effort or decrease her involvement. She and her husband, also a teacher, were both concerned how they were going to live on his teacher's salary alone, particularly as they were planning to start a family. But after praying, they both felt she should focus on her dream for A 2nd Cup.

Through expert advice on starting a nonprofit and with the financial needs of the ministry and her family being met, Erica sees that God has provided. For example, during their first year on one salary, a friend of her husband's aunt left an amount in her will to him unexpectedly—a gift equal to Erica's previous annual salary.

Giving Money When Time Is Limited: Laurie

In contrast to Erica, many women aren't able to give generously of their time because of other commitments, such as young children or a demanding job. Laurie is one. Her work as an attorney and executive in a corporate law department doesn't leave her time for volunteering.

For her, giving financially is a way of offering what God has placed in her hands.

Many women and their children live on the street as the result of events out of their control. Their homeless status may be the consequence of domestic abuse, job loss, medical expenses, or other circumstances. The current Star of Hope shelter for women serves as a safe place for such women.

When Laurie, gifted with business acumen, learned of Star of Hope's plans to build a new, larger campus, she wanted to know more. During her visit to the existing shelter, her heart broke. The rooms were tiny, each with four cots. Because of limited space, halls were often filled with pallets for overflow needs. She said with sadness, "And each resident could only bring one small bag of belongings. Imagine if that was all you had." Laurie also toured a room with pads on the walls and a punching bag to help angry youth staying at the shelter vent their frustrations. "The youth are probably not the only ones needing an outlet for anger," Laurie said as she reflected on the mothers, many of whom had experienced trauma.

Although Laurie heard many stories of women passing through that transition shelter, she remembers one story in particular: A woman was so desperate, she decided to take her life by standing on nearby railroad tracks for the next train. As a train sped toward her, the engineer saw her in time to stop. The woman entered the Star of Hope shelter distraught, saying she couldn't even succeed at committing suicide.

"I cannot imagine experiencing such desperation and despair," Laura said as she recounted this story.

The plan for a new campus interested Laurie because the goal was to help women move forward into independence, including giving them job training. She had a heart for women trying to work and care for their families.

Laurie knew she had been blessed to share with others, and she felt God leading her to give to the new Cornerstone Community campus. When she prayed for God's guidance, the amount of $50,000 came to mind. Laurie had been a supporter of Star of Hope for many years, but never at that level. After the visit to Star of Hope, she recalled a meeting she'd had with her financial adviser a few weeks before. He told her she had an extra $50,000 for giving in her Giving Plan for that year, and Laurie realized she would give those additional funds for the new campus. She remembered, "And it is not going to be near a railroad track. Instead, the new campus will be on the metro bus routes, which the women can use to go to their new jobs."

Giving Money and Time: Tracey

Tracey's giving began as a way to help one person.

She met Brandi through a prison ministry and found out a jury had convicted her of murdering her husband. Brandi maintained her innocence, despite the fact that if she had confessed to the murder, she would have had an opportunity to serve a shorter sentence. As a Christian, she would not tell a lie, even to get out of prison sooner.

Tracey regularly visits Brandi, offering encouragement and prayer. For a while, Brandi's family gave money and gifts to her. But over the years, family members died or became incapable of supporting her. The prison system's resources were limited, so she had to ration toilet paper, and she used lye soap, which was less costly than other types but harsh on her skin.

Like many Yale Law graduates, Tracey began her career at a large, prestigious law firm. At a Christian retreat, God revealed the beginning of a different plan for her legal career. Tracey continued to work for the law firm long enough to pay off her school loans and then took a 50 percent pay cut to work in the justice system. She laughed as she said, "I may be one of the few Yale Law School graduates who has deliberately chosen a path of downward mobility."

She worked as an assistant county attorney in Southern California and then took another cut to serve as a court magistrate, which allowed her to decide cases in family court. Her last step down the economic ladder came when she chose to serve as a mediator. She had discovered that her calling was to help others resolve their disputes before trial.

When asked how she managed the budget cuts, Tracey said she was blessed with contentment. "And there is no greater joy than seeing the Lord at work, especially in people's lives," she adds. That joy lights up her face.

As their relationship strengthened, Tracey was added to Brandi's approved visitors list. She spent more time with Brandi and began to send boxes of personal supplies to her friend through the prison system. Her support for Brandi began at one hundred dollars a month, but increased over time, even though Tracey's own source of income remained modest. Her giving enabled Brandi to help other women in prison, many of whom had no family or friends to support them. Brandi gave soap to a woman who frequently ran out of soap between prison allotments, causing other prisoners to shun and ridicule her.

Even when she doesn't know if she will continue to have the same level of income, Tracey continues to give to Brandi. She has witnessed God's faithfulness in providing for her and for Brandi. And she recognizes that God has brought good out of the circumstances, using Brandi to be a minister inside the prison walls.

"Is there a greater place of need than inside a prison?" Tracey asks.

Learning How to Give

Most of my adult life, I didn't appreciate the opportunity and responsibility that came with the blessing of money. When I began to search for deeper understanding and guidance, I found that most Christian books on the topic were written by men who mostly discussed the biblical basis for giving. I wondered, *How are women seeing their role in giving and doing so wisely?*

Women are in charge of an immense amount of money. We are entrepreneurs, highly paid professionals, and leaders in businesses. We are also likely to manage money alone for a significant portion of our lives. We are marrying later. Whether married or single, women are responsible for substantial financial resources.

I also searched for Christian books on *how* to give. I didn't know where to begin, but I knew I needed a plan of some type, or my giving would be impulsive, sporadic, and limited. Secular books offered advice on choosing effective organizations, but they didn't address how faith influences giving decisions. I needed an understanding of generosity from a biblical point of view, and I also needed the basic steps to giving wisely.

When Women Give is a general discussion of giving and includes the kind of advice I wanted when I began my journey. It's filled with practical advice and stories to help anyone grow in giving. In it are stories of friends and role models who faithfully and extravagantly give. I share my personal experiences, but not as one who has mastered giving; I'm still learning. I share as transparently as I can in the hope that they will be an encouragement—and sometimes make you laugh.

Why is giving important? Jesus promised that if we remain in him and his words remain in us, we will "bear much fruit" (John 15:5, 7-8). From this fruit, we will prove to the world that we, like the women Christ called to be some of his first disciples, are indeed his followers.

God is calling women to step up *now* with our financial resources as well as with our talents, skills, and time. God has placed much in our hands in order to bless others and bring glory to him.

Here is the big revelation thus far on this journey: the greater the giving, the greater the adventure, and the greater the adventure, the greater the joy.

CHAPTER 2

What God Has Placed in Women's Hands

Women have been impacting the world for good as long as history has recorded the activities of human beings. We remember Christian women like Florence Nightingale, Dorothy Day, and Mother Teresa, as well as women in Scripture, the news, and our history books. Christian women who live generously are, for the most part, everyday women who see a need, hear God speak, and respond. They are women like Erica, Laurie, and Patti.

From Time and Talent to Treasure

Historically, women have mostly served generously in churches and communities by using the gifts and talents God has given them. But women's giving has changed, because financial knowledge and management is no longer a man's world.

Doug, a successful private equity investor and manager, is excited about this role of women. His family, including his wife, grown children, and grandchildren, took a cruise as a gift from his mother. During the cruise, he asked the two younger generations to meet with him for a few hours so he could share his knowledge of investing and financial decision making. Out of all those who attended, his thirty-year-old niece was the most enthusiastic about it. For Doug, her interest was evidence of women's growing interest in financial matters.

Women today have a greater range of interests, experience, and education than in previous generations. In the United States, women began working outside the home in increasing numbers in the 1940s.[1] During the decades after World War II, women went from working in support positions, such as file clerks and administrative assistants, to becoming business leaders, entrepreneurs, and high-earning professionals. Women who are part of the baby boomer generation and the greatest generation have a net worth of over $19 trillion.[2] Today women have charge of over half of all individuals' monetary resources in the United States.[3]

In a recent survey of men and women in the workforce over the age of twenty-five, more women had college degrees than men.[4] One study of Christian women concluded they are no different. Sixty-two percent were in the workforce (compared to 59 percent at large), and 78 percent held a college degree or higher (compared to 30 percent at large).[5]

In the United States, women fill nearly 50 percent of supervisory roles and jobs requiring a college education.[6] In 2014, women made up 38 percent of all lawyers[7] and 30 percent of all doctors.[8]

In Great Britain, women physicians are expected to outnumber their male counterparts in the near future.[9] In addition, women fill almost 30 percent of the positions at the middle and upper levels in corporations in the United Kingdom.[10] Women in Great Britain have been starting their own businesses at a higher rate than men for more than two decades.[11] Firms owned by women in the United States have increased by 74 percent in fewer than twenty years.[12] In six Western countries—Portugal, Spain, Germany, Italy, the United

Kingdom, and the United States—more than 9 percent of the millionaires are women.[13]

The majority of women who marry are married for a shorter period. Those who marry are likely to wait until they are older to do so.[14] And almost 40 percent of women have not married.[15] Most women control their finances sometime during their lives, in part because women live longer than men.[16] Thus most women steward financial resources as singles at some point in their lifetime.[17]

Alongside growing opportunities for women in the workplace, a new paradigm of giving is emerging. Women now appreciate how financial resources can significantly impact an organization working to help others,[18] often on a larger scale than giving time through volunteering.

Single women are both "more likely to give, and give more" than single men.[19] Married women are also champions in giving. In a survey for *Directions in Women's Giving 2012,* in which 70 percent of the women surveyed were married, 39 percent said they were "the primary decision-maker" on giving in their homes.[20] Ninety-two percent of the participants considered themselves at least equal partners in (if not responsible for) their household's giving decisions.[21]

In *Women and Philanthropy: Boldly Shaping a Better World,* the authors, who are recognized leaders in understanding women's philanthropy, discuss the shift. They say that for most women, the underlying motivation for giving has always been to have a positive impact on others.[22] They desire to help those in their community or other communities around the world in tangible ways.[23] Today women view *treasure* as an important vehicle to impact the world.

In 2007, two sisters initiated Women Moving Millions,[24] challenging women to help other women and girls around the world financially. It has become a movement of women making gifts of $1 million or more.

The compilation of their study, *All In for Her,*[25] concluded that women in North America could contribute $224 billion each year to charitable causes if they gave only 1.7 percent.[26] Jacqueline Zehner, chief engagement officer and president of Women Moving Millions, puts this figure in perspective: the amount is "approximately equal to all charitable giving from individuals in the United States, and roughly equal to 3.3 times the overall charitable giving by foundations and corporations in the United States" in 2013.[27] And North American women are projected to have charge of over $33 trillion by 2030, with the opportunity to give almost $570 billion yearly, if they gave only 1.7 percent per year.[28]

Christian Women in the Movement of Financial Generosity

In 2013 I met Sharla and a few women from Houston to hear about their plans for a pilot event on generosity designed specifically for women. Sharla was one of the founders of a new organization, Women Doing Well, which has women's generosity as its mission. I met the cofounders, Pam and Sharon, at the event. By the end of the day, I knew God was at work in an exciting way.

How did Women Doing Well come to be?

One Saturday afternoon in December 2010, Sharon, Pam, Sharla, and a fourth cofounder, Ann, agreed to meet at Sharon's home in Atlanta. They recognized that women could play a greater role in living generously. They shared with God this burden on their hearts and sought guidance on how they could serve women.

In the basement of Sharon's house, they used a whiteboard for each person to write her individual mission, strengths, spiritual gifts, and experience. When they stepped back from the whiteboard, they stared in amazement at what each had written. Sharla described the result as a "tapestry [of gifts, skills, and talents], with each complementing the other."[29] In time, all four women left their previous work to form Women Doing Well.

The new organization initiated the first study of Christian women's giving with the Sagamore Institute and Baylor University's Faith and Religion Institute.[30] Surveys were sent to more than ten thousand women. They hoped to receive three hundred responses to have statistically sound data from which to draw conclusions, yet over seven thousand women responded. The overwhelming feedback made this survey the largest study of women's philanthropy at that time.

The main findings of the research were that the majority of women who responded felt they could give more, but they didn't have a clear understanding of their purpose or passion, and they desired more teaching on the biblical principles of giving.[31]

Women Doing Well began to promote generosity among women and to provide tools to help women give.[32] With nine additional women, they formed a team with diverse experience, talents, and gifts, but a common passion for women's generosity. They believed that God had called them together for his big plans.

Women Doing Well holds Inspiring Generous Joy events, one-day gatherings where women hear biblical teaching on giving, participate in small-group discussions, and engage in individual exercises to help them see more clearly their purpose and passion. They learn about the importance of planning for giving and begin to set goals. Women Doing Well also leads half-day workshops to go deeper into the subjects. All of these events are designed by women, held by women, and intended for women. The goal is to create a comfortable and safe environment for women to discuss money and giving with other women as peers.

The three events held in 2013 led to demand for events in other cities. The first events averaged one hundred women but grew quickly to average more than 150.

Pam Pugh, one of the founders, asks this about women's giving: "Could it be that God is resourcing women so that through their hearts and through their hands the world will experience a wave of generosity in his name?"[33]

Women's ability to give financially has grown substantially and will continue to grow in the future. Christian women are no exception. God is moving in the hearts of Christian women to embrace the opportunity to give financially. This is not a trend. This is a movement. God is on the move to give to the world through women.

CHAPTER 3

God's Invitation to Give

My giving was like many women's. I served with others in the activities of my church. Because my time was a scarce commodity, I viewed that participation as giving sacrificially. I thought I was offering the most important gift: my time. I neglected to think about giving money or about why God had blessed me with more than I needed.

The light bulb went on one day in October 2007.

Two Christian businessmen, one from my local church, invited a small group to lunch. David talked about his experience at an annual Celebration of Generosity, a gathering of Christians to learn about and reflect on living generously. He invited us to the next one, in Lost Pines, Texas. Before our lunch ended, I knew God was leading me to go.

When I arrived, I soon learned I had entered the world of those who give not just generously, but extravagantly. My reaction? These people are crazy. What they were doing freaked me out. I thought I should head back (as in *bolt* back) to Houston, where I could find reasonable Christians.

But I stayed.

Chip Ingram took the stage to teach the group about the parables of the buried treasure and the pearl of great price. In these two parables, Jesus taught that the kingdom of God is *so valuable* it is worth sacrificing *everything* for (Matthew 13:44-46). In one parable, a man found a treasure in a field and sold everything he had so he could purchase the field. In the second story, a dealer in pearls gave all he owned to buy the pearl of great price. Jesus was explaining the immense value of the kingdom of God: it's like buried treasure and a very valuable pearl. Its value is so great that it's worth giving up *everything* to have it.

I understood these parables as never before. I comprehended for the first time that giving up everything for the kingdom of God is not a sacrifice or a noble act—it's just plain smart! It's a no-brainer.

How Generous Are We?

During the event, the founder of a financial advisory firm, Ron Blue, spoke about money. I had never heard a financial adviser talk about saving, giving, and spending from a Christian point of view. When I returned to Houston, I contacted Derek, one of the firm's financial advisers.

Before Derek could help me, I needed to gather financial information. As I reviewed tax return files for each year since my first full-time job, I was surprised that there were years when I hadn't given as much to the church as I thought. I had considered myself a faithful supporter of my church—and I was rather pleased with myself for being one. But I wasn't one.

My giving outside the church was impulsive, expected, and often comparable to what I believed others were giving. I gave in response to mail solicitations, trusting that my few dollars to organizations would do some good, but also thinking, *At least I'm not risking much on them.* Even in the years when I gave to my church, I didn't give even 1 percent to ministries that served those in need.

I was not so generous after all.

I am not alone. Only about 323 million of the world's 7.3 billion people live in the United States.[1] Yet some sources estimate that 80 percent of the world's Christians' financial resources are in the hands of American Christians.[2]

But wait a minute, we may say. Why does God need us to give to meet someone else's needs? Why doesn't he just meet their needs directly?

God's Priority — You

Why does God choose to meet the needs of others through us? *Relationship*. God values relationship more than anything. As the triune God—Father, Son, and Spirit—continually dwells in love, we can say God is all about *connection*. God blesses us to bless others to foster relationships—our relationship with him and our relationships with others. When we share God's gifts to us, we become messengers of Christ, helping connect God with others.

God's giving plan is not just a one-way flow through us to those in need. Both are receiving, and both are giving. The needs of both and the opportunities to meet the needs of both create a dynamic that fosters relationships. The result is a kind of trinity among God, those with resources, and those with less (see figure 1).

Paul described this interdependence when he encouraged the church at Corinth to follow through on its previous promise to give, using the Macedonian churches as examples (2 Corinthians 8:13-15). Through this interdependence, God is glorified (9:12-13).

We Are Hardwired to Live Generously

We were made to give. Scripture tells us that God made men and women in his image (Genesis 1:26-27), so we were made to love. We were made to enjoy what our Creator enjoys. We were also made to act with authority and responsibility toward all God has created on earth and entrusted to us. We share this responsibility with each other and with God.

The story of giving is not a story of fulfilling a duty. God's desire for our steward-ship of all that he has given us reflects his desire to be present with us, sharing life together. This life is not merely existence, static and safe, but joining him in the adventure for which he made us. This is living life to the full.

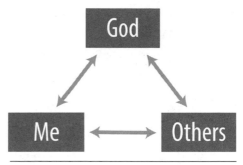

God is the ultimate giver. His giving nature is reflected in how we are created. The Holy

Figure 1. Sharing God's gifts to us connects God with others

Spirit works in us to transform our hearts so that we live with increasing generosity and its joy. Interestingly, science leads us to the same truth. Our brains are wired to experience joy when giving. In a study, scientists tracked blood flow in the brain when people acted generously. They discovered that *part of our brain lights up when we give money*.[3]

Bottom line, we experience joy when we give.

Science is not alone in revealing our penchant for giving. Our hearts also tell us so. We want our lives to have meaning. We desire to make the world a better place. We are drawn to impact others for good.

Made to Participate in God's Story

God's plan is that we use all he has given for the good of our families and church communities, but it doesn't stop there. God's plan also extends to giving for the good of others, even those we may not know. God has good deeds planned for us to do (Ephesians 2:10).

In Mark's account of Jesus' feeding of the five thousand, we see Jesus' invitation to join him in giving. The apostles came to him with a need: the crowd listening to Jesus was hungry. Jesus' response must have floored them: "You feed them."

Observe the way Jesus *immediately* involved them in meeting the needs of others. As we often do, they looked at their resources and responded, "What good can we do? This is too big."

Jesus then told them to ask those in the crowd to give what they had and bring it to him. They returned with five loaves and two fish. Blessing the loaves and fish, Jesus told the disciples to distribute the food. They returned with baskets of food as surplus.

Jesus had taken and blessed what had been given. Recognizing their limitations, they had to surrender their meager offering to Christ—who multiplied their efforts. Although Jesus performed the miracle, he required the disciples to play a servant role in helping others.

In this story, Jesus invited the disciples into his activity to meet the needs of others. As we embrace generosity, we also are swept into God's activity.

The Smartest Money Decision: Invest in the Kingdom of God

When my father died, my brother and I moved my mother into an assisted living facility in our hometown. The apartment was not large enough to hold all the possessions in our childhood home, so a lot of things had to go. My dad's favorite chair. The maple furniture they bought not long after they married. The many quilts my grandmother made. The World Book Encyclopedia my parents bought from a door-to-door salesman.

A reality check: all our stuff is headed to the same place eventually—the local landfill. All our carefully chosen wallpaper, wood floors, granite countertops, leather car seats, Apple products, and ergonomic office chairs have the same destination. And the money we have at death—well, we know the old saying "You can't take it with you."

Jesus teaches us to avoid gathering treasure in this world and to "store up" treasure in heaven (Matthew 6:19-21). The only way to lay up treasure in heaven is to invest in what has eternal value—the kingdom of God—and to be a part of God's plan for the world now.

Money Is the Strongest Rival for Our Hearts

There is another reason to live generously: money can be dangerous.

Money is a powerful rival to God. Maybe this is why Jesus taught so much about it. For example, he told a rich young man he should sell everything, give the proceeds to the poor, and follow him (Mark 10:17-29). The young man was convinced he had kept all the commandments. So why did he approach Jesus? Was he looking for affirmation or praise from Jesus when he asked, "What must I do to inherit eternal life?" (v. 17).

Jesus knew the man's idea of the kingdom of God was wrong; it was focused on a checklist of the commandments he learned as a child. He missed that the kingdom is about one's heart.

Jesus told him to sell everything and give to the poor. Why would he tell him to do something so ridiculous and almost cruel? Because he saw very clearly that money controlled the young man. The rich young ruler's situation was an emergency. He was entrapped. Jesus saw it, brought out the wire cutters, and offered radical freedom.

Jesus understood the power of money, so he told a story of a farmer planting seed. The seed is God's Word, good seed ready to grow. Yet, not all of the seed matured into plants. Jesus said, "The seed falling among the thorns refers to someone who hears the word, but the worries of this life and the deceitfulness of wealth choke the word, making it unfruitful" (Matthew 13:22).

Wealth results in unfruitfulness? Why would money interfere with the work of the Word of God in our lives? Self-sufficiency. With all our needs met and resources for other comforts, we can easily grow to depend on God less and less. We live independently though God has good deeds planned for us (Ephesians 2:10). We lose our chance to step into God's work and to work alongside him. We miss the adventure.

Our Children Are Watching

Money can also be a hazard to our children. Andrea was a typical three-year-old, complete with a strong will. She and her mother were in that common test of wills: potty training. On one occasion, Mandy was emphasizing the necessity of using the toilet. She explained, "Poo-poo needs to go in the potty."

Andrea responded, "Can't we just buy some poo-poo and put it in the potty?" Mandy realized Andrea was learning something in addition to potty training. Children learn from us, beginning at an early age. How many of us have experienced the embarrassment of a young child playing back for us (or our in-laws or pastor) something they heard us say?

The issue is not *whether* our children learn about money from us. The issue is *what* they learn. More than two thirds (67 percent) of high-net-worth parents told UBS, a financial investment firm, they felt their children took things for granted. More than half (53 percent) were at least somewhat worried that their children acted entitled. They felt their children didn't understand the value of money (65 percent), lacked motivation (54 percent), harbored unrealistic expectations (54 percent), and would embark on unstable career paths (50 percent).[4] A materialistic lifestyle can harm our children's work ethic and hurt their ability to develop compassion and empathy for others. What are our children learning as they watch us?

In Scripture, we see examples of parents who faithfully taught their children by their actions as well as their words. In Exodus, the people of God gave to the building of the tabernacle with valuable possessions God gave them as they left Egypt. Moses said to the Israelite community: "This is what the LORD has commanded: From what you have, take an offering for the LORD. Everyone who is willing is to bring to the LORD an offering of gold, silver and bronze; blue, purple and scarlet yarn and fine linen" (Exodus 35:4-6).

How did the people respond? They "brought an offering to the LORD for the work" (Exodus 35:21). How much did they bring? So much the skilled craftsmen working on the tent of meeting left their work to tell Moses they had "more than enough." The people "were restrained from bringing more" (36:6-7). Consider for a moment what their children learned about giving by watching their parents proffering valuables for the tent of meeting.

In Paul's letter to the church at Corinth, we also learn about the generosity of the Macedonians: "In the midst of a very severe trial, their overflowing joy and their extreme poverty welled up in rich generosity. For I testify that they gave as much as they were able, and even beyond their ability. Entirely on their own, they urgently pleaded with us for the privilege of sharing in this service to the Lord's people" (2 Corinthians 8:2-4). Consider what their children learned from watching their parents giving.

John and Ann, friends in my neighborhood, grew up with examples of generosity. After they married, they shared the same heart for giving. Ann tells the story of seeing her grandmother writing checks to charities that served the emotionally disabled, even though the family farm provided limited income. John recalls his mother serving on a number of nonprofit boards—as many as sixteen at one time. He said, "I have a vivid image of her with a phone to her ear" in conversation with nonprofit leaders.

What are our children learning by watching us? How do they see us use the resources God has given to us? Our actions speak louder than our words—maybe even louder than the words they hear in church or read in Scripture.

Are they learning to live generously?

PART 2

A Map for
the Journey

CHAPTER 4

Listening to God About Money

Money is simply a tool. Right? How do we use this tool? There are only three options: *We can save. We can spend. We can give.* None of these three choices is inherently good or bad. What makes money good or bad is its use.

Take saving. We all save. We may save plastic bags, boxes, rubber bands, or address labels. (When my saved items reach an embarrassing level, I call them a *collection.*) We save money too. In Proverbs, Solomon taught that saving for the future is wise (Proverbs 30:24-25). We read stories in the Bible of the need to save, such as Joseph leading the Egyptians to store up grain in anticipation of seven years of drought. We human beings are endowed with the ability to think about the future—not just to dream but also to plan. So we save for the future.

Spending is also good. We provide for our families. Jesus criticized the Pharisees for not taking care of their mothers. They used giving to the church as an excuse (Matthew 15:3-9). We also learn that God's provision is for our enjoyment as well as to meet our needs. Paul wrote the following instruction to Timothy, a young pastor:

> Command those who are rich in this present world not to be arrogant nor to put their hope in wealth, which is so uncertain, but to put their hope in God, who richly provides us with everything for our enjoyment. Command them to do good, to be rich in good deeds, and to be generous and willing to share. (1 Timothy 6:17-18)

As we decide to heed God's invitation to grow in our generosity, we face decisions. To whom do we give? There are over eighty-four thousand Christian nonprofits in the United States alone.[1] How much do we give? And when do we give?

There is no simple formula that yields a specific answer to these questions. Every step on this journey requires listening to God. We begin with prayer.

Spending time in prayer is not only the first step, but also a part of each step in the decision-making process. We must set aside distraction-free time to be present to the Holy Spirit's leading. We seek God's guidance on our giving decisions as we do on other decisions.

The more mature we are in our walk with Christ and in making giving decisions, the more we can distinguish his voice among our thoughts. Maturity requires submission to God—a complete willingness to respond wholeheartedly. He works in us to understand his ways and desires. He transforms our hearts to share his desires. As with other decisions, God chooses not to dictate to us everything we are to do. He works the same way as he cultivates generosity in us.

God doesn't want a robot-like relationship with us. He allows us to choose. His desire is that we mature in our walk with him, understanding his character and desires. But listening to God is difficult in a hurried culture.

Our Brains on Hurry

We are *busy*. The vice chancellor of the University of Oxford, Louise Richardson, a mother of three, was so focused on time management she always "keyed in 1:11, 2:22, 3:33 on her microwave rather than 1:00, 2:00 and 3:00, because hitting the same number three times took less time."[2] (Do you do this too?)

We believe multitasking is a necessary life skill. (I can put on mascara while doing almost anything.) However, science is now telling us that we can't multitask effectively.[3] Our brains aren't made for it.

We can have almost anything delivered to our home: groceries, laundry, prescriptions, new clothes, meals, and even decorated Christmas trees. We have microwaves for cooking (do we all agree this counts as cooking?), automatic sprinkler systems, and remote controls for our audiovisuals, garage doors, and security systems.

Yet, with all our time-saving strategies, we continue to live life in a hurry. We are like racecar driver Mario Andretti, who has been quoted as saying about racing, "If everything seems under control, you're just not going fast enough."

In addition, we must make more decisions. Think about the many decisions you're required to make in your favorite grocery store. The breakfast cereal industry led the charge, filling a whole aisle. The soft drink industry followed—not to mention the aisle containing bottled water. And now we have an aisle of toilet paper choices. (Really now? Just saying.)

Science tells us that we have a limited amount of energy to make decisions and exercise willpower each day.[4] In addition to addressing so many choices, we also overcommit ourselves. We don't want to disappoint someone.

For these reasons and others, we find it difficult to be still and listen for God to guide us; we often fall asleep, exhausted. So, how can we return to being present to God's voice? We have to make it a priority.

Is Hearing God a Priority?

Jesus came to the home of Mary and Martha and brought a number of disciples with him. Martha was anxiously preparing the meal when she grew frustrated with her sister Mary, who wasn't helping. Instead she was listening to Jesus as he taught. Martha sought Jesus' support, but he surprised her when he said Mary had made the better choice: being with Jesus, listening to him—even when tradition, others' expectations, and empty stomachs pressed for action (Luke 10:38-42). We can't live the life of a follower of Jesus Christ without taking time before him in silence, just listening.

God wants us to rest. He provided the Sabbath as a gift to his people, Israel, after their liberation from slavery in Egypt. They didn't know how to rest or to worship the true God, having lived as slaves before their exodus, providing labor *every* day of the week—no weekends, no vacations, and no sick days with pay. Failure to show up at the work site meant a significant risk of bodily harm.

We women can view our work both inside and outside the home as difficult to stop; it seems to require our attention seven days a week. Yet stillness and silence allow space for us to be aware of God's presence and to hear God guide us on our giving and other uses of money.

What If I Hear God Wrong?

Although we seek to give wisely as good stewards, we do so in complete freedom. Why? We aren't responsible for ensuring the outcomes of our giving. Whew, what a relief! The results are in God's hands and are his responsibility. We give in freedom, knowing that if we give with a right heart and with the wisdom and guidance God provides, he is honored and pleased. He is the one with the power to control the results and the timing of outcomes. We are called to be faithful only.

Giving us freedom, God intentionally uses the joys and challenges of giving to help us grow as disciples of Jesus and to live in complete fellowship with him. This is true even if it appears in hindsight that we didn't make the best decision. And God may be working through questionable decisions in ways we can't see.

Every Village, a ministry in South Sudan, sought gifts in 2012 to build new missionary homes near the Nuer tribe in South Sudan. I decided to contribute to the construction of one of these homes for a new missionary family. The homes and other buildings in the missionary compound in Nasir were completed in 2013. At the end of the year, civil war broke out in South Sudan. Soon the missionary families had to flee their homes and evacuate to Ethiopia, along with the local Nuer tribespeople.

Although the brokenness of the situation was overwhelming, God used it for good in an unexpected way. The experience of the South Sudanese had been that foreigners who came to serve there would always leave them when fighting or other difficulties happened. On this occasion, the missionaries suffered the same loss of homes and belongings as they did and joined them as refugees in Ethiopia. The Nasir refugees and missionaries endured hardship together. As a consequence, those from Nasir grew to trust the missionaries, who then had unparalleled access to their hearts. Relationships would have taken much longer to build otherwise. Peter, the executive director of Every Village, says, "When they see that we have not forgotten them, then they believe that God has not forgotten them."[5]

Peter and Shauna, his wife, served in South Sudan long before working with Every Village. For two years they served as a missionary couple near Mvolo. But Peter developed a heart issue, and they had to leave. Discouraged and confused, they returned to the United States. "How is God at work in this?" they asked.

When Peter's health returned, the board of Every Village invited him to serve as executive director. Every Village has since distributed over forty thousand solar-powered radios to villages and erected radio towers and stations for the local broadcasting of Bible stories, news, and health education. In addition, villages in South Sudan are enjoying clean water from the sixty-one wells drilled for them in the past few years. Eleven new missionaries have been trained and have moved to villages in South Sudan to live with the South Sudanese.

Peter and Shauna share great joy knowing that the village area they lived in as new missionaries now has twenty wells as well as one of the broadcast towers. Another milestone may come shortly when Every Village sends the first missionaries back to the village Peter and Shauna had to leave in 2005.

Did they fail to hear God correctly when they decided to serve in South Sudan in 2005? No, God just had a different plan—and different timing.

Did those who contributed to the missionary complex, which is likely now inhabited by rebel forces, make a mistake? No, I do not think so. We simply can't see God's plan beforehand. Who knows, maybe a rebel will pick up a Bible and read it.

So we wait in faith, knowing that God is at work.

CHAPTER 5

How Much Do I Give?

When I was a child, my parents made me share with my younger brother, and sometimes I felt it was unfair. After all, what I had was *mine*. I developed my own answer to the question of how much I had to give him: as little as possible. I felt he should be immensely grateful for that portion. We may subconsciously have the same philosophy when determining how much to give. The question is not how much we *have* to give, but how much we *get* to give.

So, how much do we give? Here is a straightforward way to evaluate how much to give:

What we give away = (what we have) – (what is enough)

Simple. Right?

Reflecting on the amount we need to thrive—and pledging to give away the remainder—is a spiritual exercise. We quickly learn the role that our possessions, money, and socioeconomic group play in shaping our identity. As we increase our giving, we also discover what or whom we place our security in. Because of the uncertainty of the future, we're tempted to keep more than we need. As we learn to let go, we learn to trust more deeply the one who has our future in his hands and loves us immensely.

How Much Has God Given Us?

We recognize that God's blessings are much greater than any financial blessings. God's greatest blessing is his saving grace and a relationship with him through Jesus Christ. Other blessings include family, friends, health, and provision for our basic needs. We recognize these quickly. With reflection, we can see other blessings from God.

- What are the talents, skills, education, and spiritual gifts we have been given (for example, accounting, singing, organization, leading, drawing, hospitality, language)?

- What are the intangible gifts we have received (for example, influence, relationships, stamina, and acumen)?

- What opportunities have we received (for example, employment, medical care, travel, arts, sports)?

- How have we been blessed financially (for example, salary and wages, investments, real property, retirement funds, businesses, possessions, and inheritances)?

God's immense generosity goes beyond what we know. Many times he protects us, provides for us, and acts on our behalf when we are unaware.

Gratitude is an attitude we carry with us every day. Without gratitude, we can easily believe our financial resources and other blessings are the result of our hard work and wise living. One of the powerful messages of the story of Job is that we receive *everything* as a generous gift from God.

God has blessed many of us with the ability and opportunity to work and earn money. We use our time and talent in our daily work, where we experience and share God's love and contribute to the common good. During certain seasons in our lives, we may have a limited capacity to give time and talent, such as when we have young children at home or elderly parents to care for, or when we are working on business deals or major projects at the office or other work.

In his book *The Eternity Portfolio, Illuminated*, Alan Gotthardt writes:

> If earning that money—while following the Spirit's leading in your priorities—keeps you from volunteering as much of your time, don't be "guilted" into giving up the stage God has called you to in the mistaken belief that only "hands-on ministry" matters. We don't need everyone playing on the same stage. We need all Christians serving *primarily* in their God-given roles.[1]

Whether our workplace is inside or outside the home, the more we make ourselves available to God, the more we can give our time and talent to God in that location. And we can give financially to ministries.

Have you heard the phrase "time, talent, and treasure"? Is it surprising that this phrase isn't in Scripture? Certainly Scripture teaches us to do good deeds and use our gifts. But from the *order* of "time, talent, and treasure," we can believe incorrectly that the greater gifts are time and talent. Interestingly, Scripture contains much more about giving money than about giving time or talent. Could that be because giving financially is more of a challenge?

Scripture teaches that we are to give, so each of us begins with the question, do I know what financial resources God has placed in my hands? What is the total value of the resources in my possession, less any debt I owe?

When I was in college, my resources included the value of a 1960 Ford Galaxie 500, a twin bed, a small desk, a table and chairs that had belonged to my grandmother, and various kitchen and bathroom hand-me-downs, plus cash from summer jobs, and a few scholarships. (I thought I was rich.) From that total, I subtracted the outstanding debt (student loans), and that number was my financial net worth. At that time, my net worth was a large number—a large *negative* number.

For most of us, determining our net worth requires a bit more. It may include the amount in bank accounts, investments, cash value of insurance policies, real estate, ownership interests, collections, antiques, and other things with material value. From this total value, we subtract outstanding debt, such as mortgages or credit card debt. The final result is our financial *net worth*.

After we determine our net worth, we should consider expected future additions. These may be salary, revenue from investments, or future assets we expect to receive, such as a pension, an inheritance, or Social Security.

Along with future additions, we will incur future expenses. Our expenses will change during our lifetimes, reflecting life stages and alterations in circumstances, such as retirement, health, our children's college education, and help in old age.

Many of us would be confident in doing this to determine our net worth—it's simple math, right? But I'm convinced that most men and women would benefit from the help of a financial adviser. In addition, few of us set aside the time to do it, even if we enjoy it. Seeking the advice of a professional *Christian* financial adviser is wise. We need one who has a biblical perspective regarding money.

Numbers, Graphs, and Charts

Susan is a senior manager at one of the world's largest corporations. Her father was a math professor at Rice University. He would teach (or test) his daughters with math questions on occasion. He periodically asked, "If everyone at this dinner table toasts each other with a click of the glass, how many clicks would there be?" She memorized the formula: N x (N-1) divided by 2, with N as the number of people at the dinner table. Susan was uncomfortable performing the calculation in her head, because she believed she hadn't inherited her father's math skills. Yet today she manages a multimillion-dollar budget in her job. Like many other women of material net worth, she has learned to master finances, including her personal resources.

In a recent study conducted by Fidelity, only 47 percent of women were confident talking about money matters—almost half of us.[2] But the other half is not. Various reasons exist for this. We may lack an interest, or we may lack an opportunity to learn. We may have received the erroneous message early in life that women are naturally deficient in understanding financial matters.[3] Yet many of us excel at financial matters.

Regardless, we have responsibility for financial decisions and resources—or we will. God wouldn't place resources in our hands if he weren't going to provide for us to be wise stewards.

Increasing our understanding and confidence may require education. Women are good at self-education; we've taught ourselves how to use three remotes at the same time, bake a cake, and set up a tent. (And we may be the only ones who can read a set of instructions.) How did we do this? We read. We found resources online. We learned from others.

When we consider money decisions, both men *and* women need to develop a certain understanding level. For some of us, this is interesting and enjoyable. For the rest of us, it's like flossing teeth: not fun, but necessary. So with respect to money skills, we would be wise to educate ourselves, if we haven't already, *and* to seek the help of experts.

Even if we're able to do the work, we may not want to. Sometimes we hire someone to do it. I don't want to clean my chimney or fix my plumbing problems either. I need experts to help me with these, just as I need a financial adviser.

The search for a Christian financial adviser who is a good fit is a smart investment. My previous adviser thought I would blindly trust him to handle matters and offered limited explanations of his conclusions. Another one made a mistake on my income tax return, because she failed to listen. Ouch. Another provided reports containing errors, which he dismissed as inconsequential to the bottom-line conclusion. When another financial adviser passed me off to a junior employee for handling, I started a search for a new one.

So I've had disappointing experiences with some financial advisers, but generally the interest and ability to serve women is increasing. Persevere in finding one that meets your expectations.

Many financial advisers, both men and women, welcome the opportunity to teach us what we need or want to learn. They seek to communicate in the best way based on individual needs. For example, if you don't like graphs and charts as a communication tool, you can just tell your adviser. If you want more or less detail, you can speak up. If you need refreshers on the material, ask to review it again. (My financial adviser knows that I can remember my high school best friend's phone number but have limited memory of the numbers in my financial plan.)

Choosing a financial adviser is one of the most important financial decisions we can make, because he or she will disciple us in a philosophy of money—either the world's or Christ's. The Christian way of life is countercultural, especially when it comes to money. We need advice on saving, spending, *and* giving based on biblical principles.

Kingdom Advisors, one resource for finding a Christian financial adviser, is an association of Christian financial professionals "who want to integrate their faith with their practice" (kingdomadvisors. com). Members include professional financial advisers, tax advisers, and estate planning attorneys. We can also seek recommendations from friends who share our values.

How Much Is Enough?

We *know* when we have enough of some things, such as Internet passwords, emails, promotional coffee mugs, and free address labels. We often have a sense of what is sufficient, even with respect to things we buy. We know when we have enough toothbrushes, tires, raincoats, and automobile jumper cables. (My dad gave jumper cables as a gift to my mom on her birthday, which was one too many in her opinion.) With other items, it may be difficult deciding what is enough: umbrellas, reading glasses, and chocolate. Money is the most challenging. How much is enough?

After my attendance at the Celebration of Generosity, I realized I didn't know how I was using money. I gathered my credit card statements and checkbook register for the most recent year and created a list of expense categories. Then I tallied the amount spent in each category for the most recent year. (If you like details, a form to help determine expenses can be found in appendix B.)

When I completed this exercise, I discovered some interesting spending habits. For instance, I spent more on my hair than on my clothes. I was spending more on my dog's annual health exam than mine. (Next year she's going to my doctor.) I was also surprised at the amount I spent eating out, on sports tickets, and on a particular weakness of mine: books. None of these purchases are bad. God has given us things to enjoy, but the question is, how much is enough?

I also learned that what I gave to ministries was paltry compared to what I spent on comfort, convenience, and pleasure. I tried justifying some as necessities. Expenses on appearance: necessary to meet work expectations. Expenses for vacations and entertainment: indispensable for physical and mental health. Again, these activities aren't bad, but as is often the case, the issue was whether my spending on them was moderate or excessive.

After this inventory, I dropped my season tickets to the local professional baseball team. (How was I to know they would soon have a Cy Young Award–winning pitcher?) I cut back on books when I realized I owned more than I could finish in several years. (I've heard a rumor there's a library in town—somewhere.) Some or all of these may be viewed as moderate expenses compared to multiple homes, cars, entertainment systems, jewelry, the latest technology, vacations, and other more expensive items. Yet the same principle applies: how much is enough?

God created a people of his own and blessed them to be a blessing to others (Genesis 12:2). We read of God's heart breaking when his people forget the poor (Isaiah 58). Jesus also taught the importance of giving generously to the poor (Matthew 19:21). God hasn't changed his ways. His people continue to be called to give generously to others. We are to provide for and bless our families. Yet we are not to consume all our financial blessings from God without considering the needs of others.

C. S. Lewis said, "If our expenditure on comforts, luxuries, amusements, etc., is up to the standard common among those with the same income as our own, we are probably giving away too little."[4]

CHAPTER 6

What Are My Values in Choosing Organizations to Give To?

As we begin to grow in our generosity, we learn quickly that who we are influences our giving decisions. One of the greatest influences is our personal values or standards.

When we buy a car, what's important to us? Room to carry golf clubs? Space for two car seats? Leather seats? A super sound system? Rearview camera? The color? We each value different things. On the other hand, we also agree on other items: brakes, safety belts, and windshield wipers (and a powerful air conditioner if we live in Houston). As we make many decisions, we apply our values to those decisions.

As we consider who to give to, we begin with our values and how they apply to a ministry or organization. What are our most important criteria—those characteristics that, if missing, make an organization less attractive than others or even unacceptable? Some values are more important to us than others as we make decisions.

Our values show up in many decisions. For example, some place a high value on risk and adventure as they choose vacations and employment. Others place a higher value on certainty and predictability. They take vacations at well-known tourist spots and work for well-established businesses.

In our consideration of various ministries, we need to learn the organization's core values. Are they consistent with the values we believe are fundamental? (To help you discern this, see the list of values in appendix D. Circle your top ten and then list those in order of importance.) Consider questions you might ask a ministry to discover whether it views your values as important. Narrowing your list to a few and prioritizing them doesn't mean other values are not good ones. It's a matter of prioritization. The time to discover that an organization doesn't share your most significant values is before a donation, not after—particularly if it's a large donation.

Scripture-Based Standards

Are the actions of a ministry toward those it serves and its employees, contractors, and volunteers (including donors) consistent with Jesus' command to love God and to love others as we love ourselves? Here are a few things to watch for when evaluating a ministry:

Treats all with respect as made in the image of God. Steve Corbett and Brian Fikkert lead the Chalmers Center and wrote *When Helping Hurts: How to Alleviate Poverty Without Hurting the Poor . . . and Yourself.*[1] The authors discuss an unintended consequence of charity: perpetuating feelings of shame in those suffering from poverty.[2]

Corbett and Fikkert share a World Bank study that asked people in financial poverty to describe their experiences of poverty. They said they experienced not only financial poverty, but also an identity tied to poverty: "Poor people typically talk in terms of shame, inferiority, powerlessness, humiliation, fear, hopelessness, depression, social isolation, and voicelessness."[3] The authors maintain that those in poverty have difficulty accepting they are beloved children of God.[4] When we provide handouts, we reinforce what they often feel about themselves—that they are helpless and inferior.

Corbett and Fikkert propose a distinct definition of poverty. First, poverty is inherently relational. Everyone—the economically disadvantaged and the wealthy—are broken and poor, a state only Jesus can heal.[5] All human beings are uniquely gifted, so we are to work alongside those in financial poverty to support them in using their God-given abilities to provide for their families and to live out their purpose.[6] The poor must be active in the poverty alleviation process.[7]

Before understanding this perspective, I held a mistaken belief that those with money and education held the solutions to poverty. When I worked alongside those in poverty, God exposed the lie that they are helpless and incapable. God also enables those of us with more financial resources to see ourselves as broken and poor in other ways (such as spiritually). Working together, we experience God's transformation.

Other questions to consider:

- Does the ministry work within the local culture and with the local population and church in making decisions and planning activities?

- Does the ministry desire to learn from and be served by the community it seeks to serve?

Has nothing to hide. Christian organizations are almost always willing to answer questions or provide information. If they're reticent, their reluctance may be a red flag. Some information on personnel is subject to privacy laws, but most other information should be available. Ask why they're reluctant to share information. Absent a compelling reason, be concerned.

Will ministry representatives talk candidly about disappointments? About what has gone wrong? About what they have learned and how they are applying that learning?

Serves and shares. Some Christian organizations focus either on evangelism *or* on service to the neglect of the other. We need to consider this question in light of Scripture: How can we share God's love with others if we don't demonstrate love with our actions? Yet our mission is not merely to alleviate suffering. Jesus demonstrated God's love to others with his actions, but he also spoke of the coming of the kingdom of God, calling people to him and teaching them to follow him. Consider asking questions to understand whether an organization is intentional about one or both and whether the philosophy is consistent with Scripture. For example, do activities include a plan for discipleship—for those being served as well as the staff of the ministry? (Few organizations intentionally disciple their own staff and volunteers.)

What About Giving to Secular Organizations?

Donors often contribute to their university alma mater. I understand why. I'm very grateful for my undergraduate and law school education, and student loans and scholarships played a significant role in my ability to attend.

Universities and colleges receive significant dollars in grants and donations.[8] Yet some of them seem to seek to discredit Christianity in the classroom and promote values contrary to Christian ones. Thoughtfulness and due diligence is warranted before giving to an alma mater. Find out how the institution's practices have changed since you were in the classroom.

Supporting or establishing a specific scholarship fund, funding ministries that prepare or support students in college, and giving to ministries that seek to share the Christian faith with students may be good alternatives in some circumstances.

Other secular organizations support the arts or advocate for the protection of the environment. For example, giving to a zoo (a good one) or an animal rescue or adoption agency supports God's desire that we steward the earth wisely, as does giving to environmental preservation organizations. But as with other organizations, find out whether their activities are consistent with biblical standards.

Our expectations of ministries are heavily influenced by the standards or values we apply to them as we evaluate them. Ask questions to discern in advance whether a ministry is a good fit for you. You'll want to know if they are good at the work they do.

What else should you consider?

CHAPTER 7

What Is My God-Given Purpose and Passion?

Ann is an introvert with a warm smile and welcoming demeanor. You wouldn't know she's part of the fight against oppression.[1] She also shares a passion with her husband: preventing genocide. Their contributions to ministries go largely to these causes. Ann discovered as a young adult that she wanted to support those courageously bringing hope to others.

Her purpose of bringing hope is revealed in two passions. First, she gives to ministries outside the United States that serve and rescue the oppressed, such as International Justice Mission. She gives to small ministries, often startups. For example, she supports a woman who started a ministry in East Congo to come alongside rape victims.

Ann also brings hope by living out her vocation. She works as a counselor seeking to match college-bound students with the college that provides the best environment for them. She also serves with a foundation that provides college counseling to high school students who can't afford it. With both pursuits, she brings hope to others.

She is living out her unique, God-given purpose and passion.

Our Unique Design

We are each unique—not just in appearance, but in many other ways. A friend likes her cereal bowls in a certain order on the shelf. Another has watched a favorite movie so many times she can recite the dialogue. Another can hit the high notes in an opera. (You would not want me to even try.) We are all made differently.

The psalmist wrote that God knows us and forms us in the womb (Psalm 139:13). Jesus said God knows the number of hairs on our head (Matthew 10:30). (So he is aware of my thin spots.) No two of us are made alike. We have unique DNA and distinct fingerprints. And all of us have a special way we are to join God in what he is doing in the world.

Jesus said we are chosen as his followers for a purpose: "You did not choose me, but I chose you and appointed you so that you might go and bear fruit—fruit that will last" (John 15:16). Those of us who were never chosen for a sports team understand the significance of being chosen. What is the "fruit that will last"? That which has *eternal* significance.

Each of us also has a specific purpose, a part in God's story we're designed to live out. God has uniquely equipped us for that purpose with spiritual gifts, talents, and abilities. We are then shaped by or given such things as influence, financial resources, experiences (both good and bad), education, training, relationships, community, and culture. Understanding these helps us to understand God's unique purpose for us.

How is our purpose relevant to our giving? We want to give our time in areas related to our purpose. Doing so makes us feel like we're in our "sweet spot." As we devote our time and abilities to ministries serving in a certain manner, we begin to see up close the needs of others and God's heart for them. Our service with a particular ministry may provide an opportunity to see closely the organization, its leaders, and the impact of the ministry.

How do we each discern our purpose? We remain attentive to what God may be showing us about ourselves. We experience joy when we do something we feel made to do. When are we so engrossed in what we're doing that time just flies by? How have others affirmed how we do something? What do we do naturally that others don't?

I admired Becky's communication skills and sense of humor. She could combine words to touch both the heart and the head. Over coffee one morning, she shared that God had taken her on a winding path to discover her purpose, which was raising financial resources for Christian ministries. A smile broke out on her face when a surprised look appeared on mine. "Fundraising?" I responded. "You like fundraising? I thought your thing was serving in leadership in the pro-life movement."

"No," she said. "My participation in a pro-life ministry is just the way God showed me my *real* purpose." She leaned forward to explain. "I *love* helping others channel their resources for the good of the kingdom of God."

Our purpose becomes clearer as we try certain activities. My summer jobs in college were good at showing me what I shouldn't do to earn a living. Engaging on a limited basis in different means of service can help us understand how we are uniquely wired.

Another way to discern our purpose is through journaling. If you enjoy writing, try the following exercise: Record activities that give you life as well as undertakings that drain you or make you feel out of your element. Whether the activities validate our purpose or point us in another direction, the experience will help us understand how we're designed.

These questions may also be helpful:

- What are you doing now (or have done in the past) that gives you joy?

- When have you felt that you were doing what you were made to do?

- What do others tell you you're good at?

- What can you do for hours, and time passes without notice (other than soaking in a bubble bath)?

- What activities, skills, or talents do you have?

The Passion We Share with God

Beyond giving us each a unique design, God has placed in our hearts a passion he shares with us. This passion may also be a guide to our giving.

We each have interests we care greatly about. Growing up in Alabama, I developed a passion for college football. I went to my first University of Alabama football game early in life, and I followed college football before I followed Jesus.

I have two friends who are passionate followers of the royal family in England. Others are fervent about their exercise routine. My mother is ardent about a bed being made correctly. I don't share any of these passions.

Our God is a passionate God. He is passionate about us—every one of us. He holds in his heart the whole world. As we know, passion for someone can lead to pain. So God also mourns at the brokenness and evil in the world.

With the Holy Spirit residing in us, we share God's passion and pain for the world. Our passion may be connected to a group that we empathize with. Or it may be connected to something that makes us angry.

We may have a passion for a particular group of people, such as teenagers or refugees or teenagers.

We may have a passion for others experiencing a life-changing event or experience.

We may have a passion for initiating new ventures when we see a need is not being met.

We may have a passion for helping existing ministries with leadership development, planning, efficiencies, or expansion, using the skills we've learned.

We may have a passion for the hungry, because we know what it's like to go without meals. Or we may have a passion for those looking for employment, because we know what it's like to be unemployed.

Our passion is what moves our *heart* for others. It is a desire for rescue, transformation, or change that we share with God. What stirs us is no coincidence. God has placed it in our heart.

Nehemiah had a heart for the people of Jerusalem. At the beginning of the book that bears his name, he asked several visitors returning from the city, occupied by Persia, how those remaining in Jerusalem were doing. When he heard their report, he broke down and wept.

And he decided he must do something. He obtained the permission of the king of Persia to go to Judah, gather the necessary supplies, and lead a group to Jerusalem (Nehemiah 2:1-17).

Nehemiah had a passion for those left behind in Jerusalem. The report of their conditions and the condition of the temple led him to tears. Our passion evokes emotion. The emotion may be anger, sadness, frustration, empathy, or even joy or satisfaction. His passion led him to take action—to do something. During a time in prayer, he felt God's direction for him to lead a group to help those in Jerusalem.

Responding to God required a major change in Nehemiah's life. For example, he may never have been to Judah before. As a cupbearer for the king, he may never have spent weeks or months on a horse, traveling a great distance.

Often God picks the least likely candidate for an assignment, valuing his or her heart over what the world sees. When we say yes, God provides a way forward. Nehemiah received needed materials and passage from the king. He made the trip successfully (with some new equestrian skills—and calluses) and served as an important leader in Jerusalem.

What do you care deeply about?

One day I attended a local National Christian Foundation lunch. The guest speaker was a tall, thin, blond young man who could hardly stand still, he was so excited about helping the poor through microfinance. Peter, the president and CEO of HOPE International, had only a few minutes to describe the organization's mission and foundational beliefs. Some of the things he said resonated with me: respecting personal dignity, recognizing that every person is made in the image of God, and sharing God's love through our actions and through introducing them to Jesus Christ.

On the way out the door, I picked up a copy of the book *The Poor Will Be Glad* that Peter coauthored.[2] I finished it before I fell asleep that night. I learned that most of those helped through microfinance are women raising children alone after the death of or abandonment by a husband. Each woman had the desire and ability to work and care for her family.

One of the countries Peter mentioned was the Democratic Republic of Congo. *Where is that?* I wondered. Returning to work, I stopped at a bookstore to buy a world map. Did you know there are two Congos in Africa? I didn't. I pondered how I could be so involved in the local church and know so little about God's world and what he's doing in it.

I continued to read in books and online about the impact of poverty in the world. My heart broke when I read that every day the equivalent of an airliner full of children die from preventable causes.[3] If such a crash killed that many children, I'd be glued to the television news reports and crying buckets. I also learned, however, God is at work in powerful ways in response to prayer and partnership with those serving people in poverty. I had lived most of my life ignorant of and indifferent to the majority of the world.

Your passion may arise from a personal experience. Many women who have left abusive relationships give to ministries helping similar women and children. Individuals freed from addictions often seek to help others on the recovery path. For some of us, the power of someone believing in us when we were young motivated us to work with young people. Some of us support educational opportunities for students who can't afford college because we received financial support from others for our own education.

Amy, whom I met at a Generous Giving event, has passion that was sparked on an overseas trip. When she completed her MBA, she pursued her interest in business on Wall Street. When she married her husband, the only thing she brought was a television and a bedspread.

When their financial resources began to increase, they ignored it. As a consequence, they didn't change their lifestyle much. Their children weren't aware of their wealth. They wanted to be good stewards, but they felt ill-equipped to make wise giving decisions. Giving felt like a burden at times, and they didn't have peers to discuss it with.

On a one-day layover in Doha, on a trip with her daughter to Kenya, God confirmed Amy's passion for the Muslim world. Although they visited Coptic Christians, she saw the needs of many Muslims. She now works with others in the Middle East, ministering to the great needs in the area. Amy went from being a burdened and frustrated giver to one full of purpose and joy.

Many find their passion because they want to be like someone they admired. Betty, a retired elementary school teacher, has a heart for the elderly. Her passion for them developed when she was young as she accompanied her grandmother in visiting the elderly in her hometown. Betty thought it funny when her grandmother referred to them as "old." She thought her grandmother *was* old.

Some individuals like to help others experience the same opportunities they did, popularly called "paying it forward." Sarah, a partner in a financial advisory firm, has a passion for enabling children to attend Christian summer camps, because such annual visits made a major impact on her life. The Christian counselors set an example that left a big impression on her.

Jacki Zehner, CEO and president of Women Moving Millions, wanted to help women and girls. Her passion to come alongside women began during her years at Goldman Sachs.

Drew Houston, the founder of Dropbox, described passion perfectly: "The happiest and most successful people ... [are] obsessed with solving an important problem, something matters to them. They remind me of a dog chasing a tennis ball."[4]

Appendix C includes a list of potential passions that may be helpful in identifying your own. You may find it most helpful to strike out the passions you are the least passionate about until you arrive at a handful to explore.

You may also find the following questions helpful in discerning your passion:

- What evokes emotion in you when you read or hear the news?
- What makes you react immediately with a response like "someone should do something"?
- What evils, suffering, or struggles are you praying for?
- What difficulties have you experienced that have led to empathy for others facing similar situations?
- What life transformations bring you joy when you see them in others?

Some resources to help in discovering your purpose and passions are included in appendix A.

God's Plan Is Beyond Our Imagination

God has repeatedly shown that he can use all of us in his plans *if* we are fully surrendered. He enjoys choosing the least likely to be chosen by the world's standards. In doing so, others can see that he is at work (1 Corinthians 1:27-31). So God may just choose to surprise us.

Consider how we might see little evidence of how God would use these saints from Scripture:

- Peter and John, two fishermen from a small town subject to the Roman Empire—as founders of a new movement that would outlive and outgrow the empire

- Paul, a *Jewish* scholar—to preach to the *Gentile*s?

- Nehemiah—who had no experience as a soldier or a builder

- Moses—a murderer, fugitive, shepherd—to be the liberator and leader of a group of complaining former slaves going to an unknown country

- David—the runt among a family of boys, full of passion (and we know where that led), with previous experience as a shepherd and musician—to be king of Israel

- Mary, a teenage girl from a backwater town in the occupied territory of the Roman Empire—to be the mother of Jesus

- Matthew, a tax collector—to share the gospel of God's love in Christ

- Rahab, a prostitute—to assist the Israelites in capturing a city

When we look at this list, we're tempted to ask, what *was* God thinking? In so many ways, God's ways are not our ways.

Often God's assignment may be to teach us something new in areas not always consistent with our known abilities or interests. We often discover something about ourselves or about God that we didn't know.

That's part of the adventure.

CHAPTER 8

Where Can I Find Information on Organizations?

The leader of a ministry spoke at my church about the ministry's work in a country in Central America, describing poignantly the plight of the poor in the region. I later asked him by email, "What would your organization do with a large (specific) donation?"

He replied, "We would like to use a portion to send one of our faithful local volunteers on a trip to the Holy Land."

What? I thought. If I were going to send someone to the Holy Land, that person was going to be *me*. Certainly the ministry leader's desire wasn't bad, but his response raised questions about priorities and decision making in this ministry. I was glad I asked the question.

The money we give to one ministry we can't give to another. (Am I not a financial whiz?) Multiple organizations might be conducting the same type of ministry in the same geographic area. Giving to better ministries encourages less-efficient and less-effective ministries either to improve or to quit, allowing more money to go to the better ones.

Part of our stewardship is to avail ourselves of available information and to pray for wisdom and guidance. But where do we even begin to gather information about nonprofits or the areas in which they serve? We can make giving decisions confidently—not that we will always be pleased with a decision we make, but we will be confident that God knows our heart in giving and will bless us for our faithfulness and our trust in him.

Giving—and wisely doing so—takes time and effort. My efforts to find shortcuts, quick answers, and a formula to follow led to failure. In part, this failure is the result of failing to build relationships with those who influence our decisions.

However, some information resources exist and can assist us and save us time. They serve as a good starting point and can provide information so we can contact nonprofits directly. Begin with the ministry's website, where you'll probably find the ministry's mission, its history, its mission, and information on its leaders. Some ministries also provide information on the financial health of the organization and its strategic plans for the future. I'm most impressed with and appreciative of them.

Ministry leaders know that stories are effective in conveying their ministry's impact. Studies have concluded that human beings are more moved by stories than by numbers indicating the magnitude of the need or a ministry's impact. Stories help us to understand the human experience and the services offered.

It's also good to look for media reports on organizations and their leaders. I've been surprised to learn of litigation and investigations into an organization through media. And it's wise to read about other organizations doing similar work. What distinguishes a particular ministry from others performing the same activity?

A number of organizations help donors evaluate nonprofits by providing helpful information. Charity Navigator (charitynavigator .org) researches nonprofit organizations and assigns a score based on their accountability and transparency, as well as their financial health. Its long-term goal is to assess the effectiveness of an organization in having the desired impact. The site has information on over eight thousand nonprofits as well as articles and tips for donors.

The Better Business Bureau's Wise Giving Alliance (give.org) evaluates charities and has developed standards for organizations in order to promote good conduct.

The American Institute of Philanthropy, or CharityWatch (charity watch.org), evaluates organizations and publishes the *Charity Rating Guide & Watchdog Report* for donors. It also provides guidance to donors.

GuideStar (guidestar.org) maintains a database of the IRS Form 990s that each nonprofit must file with the IRS annually. In 2001, it began publishing an annual report on the compensation of non-profit leaders. It also provides information on causes that donors may be interested in.

GiveWell (givewell.org) identifies top-rated charities after re-viewing organizations' efficiency and impact based on a rigorous study. The charities they evaluate seek to help the poor and have been studied regularly to ascertain impact. GiveWell's focus is to identify the top organizations that have high impact on the greatest number of people. They also provide information on the methods of service that are most effective in meeting a need.

Another resource is the Evangelical Council for Financial Ac-countability (ecfa.org). Use its website to find organizations in a category of ministry that meet the ECFA's financial standards. The ECFA also provides resources on nonprofit governance, legal require-ments, and sound financial management. If a Christian nonprofit is not part of the ECFA, one of the first questions we want to ask is, why not?

At Barnabas Group (barnabasgroup.org) meetings, which can be found in many cities, women and men in business have the opportunity to hear ministry leaders describe their ministry activities and missions. The leaders share specific challenges in their ministries and ask for wisdom, support, and partnership from the Christian business community. The Barnabas Group prescreens the ministries presenting at meetings. Attending Barnabas Group meetings will expose you to ministries you may be interested in as well as to others who are seeking to help ministries.

You also have the opportunity to meet others who are seeking to grow in their generosity and give wisely at events hosted by the National Christian Foundation (nationalchristian.com) and Water-Stone (waterstone.org). Sometimes local groups hold events so donors can hear from certain ministries.

We can also gather recommendations from donors who are further along on their journey of growing in generosity. A good place to start is the local church. But we need to know the degree to which the church or donor has reviewed each ministry's efficiency and effectiveness. Sometimes I find that others give to a ministry as the result of a relationship or a member's request, but the ministry hasn't been adequately vetted.

Generous Giving (generousgiving.org) and The Gathering (the gathering.com) are national meetings of Christians focused on giving. Generous Giving seeks to inspire radical generosity, whereas The Gathering promotes Christian philanthropy among individuals, families, and foundations. At both of these events, we can meet others who share an interest in giving and potentially find others who share our passion for a certain need. As with local churches and friends at church, find out the degree to which they looked into a ministry before you choose to give.

Giving a small donation to an organization usually means being added to its mailing list. The organization may send materials offering insight into its goals and activities.

Our first face-to-face contact is likely to be with a development representative. Expect them to know how money is used and whether the organization is meeting its goals. I enjoy asking staff of the ministries about their own faith journey, including why they joined the ministry.

As your giving to an organization increases, meet with the leaders or talk with them by phone so you learn about the organization's leadership, finances, strategic plans, and impact. Each of us needs to decide what level of gift necessitates that further review. In some cases, the review may be appropriate because of a recurring gift that will continue for a certain length of time.

The greater the amount we give, the more we should know about the ministry and its impact. Begin by considering the ministry's leadership, but consider other questions as well.

CHAPTER 9

How Do I Identify a Good Organization?

Few of us walk into a dealership, point at a car, and agree to purchase it without examining it first. We drive it, ask questions, and do some research online. We talk to friends or car buffs. We perform similar investigations when we buy a house, select a school for our children, replace our smartphone, or make other significant decisions.

Doesn't our giving merit the same degree of research and review?

Asking questions before giving is wise. God can use our investigation of organizations to teach us how to give more wisely and to walk in faith. And understanding a ministry's work better can help us see how God is at work in the world, which is exciting.

There are limits to our ability to assess organizations. But the greater the amount we give, the more we should seek information and understanding. Check them out; perform due diligence.

Seek information from others who have previously performed due diligence, such as another donor or the organizations named in the previous chapter. However, don't assume that because people have given to an organization, they have done due diligence—not even your church, unfortunately. Inquire about what research has been done. (Due diligence on the due diligence?)

Good organizations focus on conducting their activities with excellence. Excellence is generally demonstrated by efficiency *and* effectiveness—or said another way, wisely using resources and maximizing impact.

So, what should we look for?

Strong Leadership

As one adviser to donors said, "Learn early in the process that you are investing in people, not ideas or organizations."[1] The leadership of a ministry is critical to its success.

Leadership begins at the top with the board of directors. They are responsible for the financial health of the organization and its strategic direction. Ask about the board: who serves on it, how were they selected, and what is their experience. The board should be actively engaged in strategic planning, major decisions, and financial management. It also should not be running day-to-day operations. It should meet regularly (at least twice a year). Where does it meet? (If it's Hawaii, ask to join the board.)

Board members are expected to support the mission financially. Do all board members give financially to the ministry in a significant manner? If board members are not committed to the ministry sufficiently to make it a priority in their giving, are they the best members for the board?

Do the board members have the experience to provide leadership and strategic thinking? Family members and friends of the board's founder may have good intentions, but they may not be qualified. The best board members have experience in leadership, finances, or strategic planning. Professional experience (law, accounting, theology, human resources) is helpful in governing the organization.

The organization's bylaws should provide the process for election of directors. To ensure directors on the board don't settle in and grow weary or complacent, the bylaws should provide term limits.

Even though the president may have a powerful vision, the board has a fiduciary responsibility to the organization to set and maintain the mission and the strategy. The best organizations have boards that ask tough questions, share opinions in candid discussions, and make clear decisions.

If you plan to give a substantial gift, don't be reluctant to talk to the leaders of the organization directly. I enjoy meeting the president or a board member and hearing that person's perspective. Of course I'm not talking about organizations the size of World Vision. Honestly, though, I suspect Richard Stearns, the president of World Vision, would be willing to talk with me if I asked. The organizations that receive the greatest percentage of my giving annually are those that have a president that's willing to talk regularly and who gives candid answers to questions.

How long has the president been with the organization? What is the president's training and experience? How did the president come to the organization? Has that position had significant turnover?

Often a founder serves as the president or the board chair. The founder's participation often helps with maintaining focus on the mission. Yet, on occasion, the founder is the individual that other board members defer to or who wants to control strategic decisions inappropriately.

Strategic Planning

A strategic plan provides for *how* the organization will achieve its mission. Strategic plans should be prepared for the short term (one year) and for the long term (three to ten years). Good organizations have a *process* for developing these plans.

A strategic plan is more than a list of goals. Generally, a good plan incorporates the "how" of reaching each goal. It discusses how progress will be measured, what resources will be needed, and how success will be determined.

As you review a strategic plan, consider these questions:

• Are the goals specific enough to know when they have been met?

• Are the goals focused on the mission or on opportunities beyond the stated mission?

• How does the organization plan to achieve the goals?

• Is the ministry taking reasonable risks to expand or test innovative methods?

• Does any plan for expansion include the needed resources?

• Is the organization identifying and managing the risks inherent in its activities? Many risks can't be eliminated, but can be reduced.

• Is faith used to justify weak planning and a lack of strategic thinking?

Financial Management

Does the ministry have strong financial management? Every organization needs processes to ensure that the right people provide input and approve expenditures. The higher the amount of an expense, the higher the position of the person in the organization who approves it. Before a leader approves an expense, others familiar with the organization's purpose and details should endorse it as appropriate for payment. Good financial management also includes having good processes for making decisions on savings and investments.

A ministry I became interested in served in a creative way, making college loan payments for graduating seniors during the period they agreed to serve on the mission field. The founder of the organization served on the board and had assumed the role of managing the investment of donations received to support candidates for a set number of years. He had made a significant amount of money from these investments and believed he was knowledgeable.

All went well until 2008, when the stock market dropped drastically in value. So did the ministry's ability to support those serving on the mission field for the agreed period. Those familiar with prudent investing recognize that investing so much in the stock market when moneys are going to be needed in the next few years is unwise, regardless of the performance of the stock market up to that point. It would have been prudent to invest conservatively to ensure that the donated funds were available in the short term.

From this experience, I learned that when I make a commitment to give regularly over a period beyond one year or for use beyond one year, I need to ask how the funds will be used and when, and how the funds will be invested or saved. Also, a ministry should have such processes, and accounts should be separate from the personal accounts of any individual or other organization.

Here are some helpful questions to ask about an organization's finances:

- Has the organization had any occurrences of fraud, cash-flow problems, or problems that might indicate weak financial processes and controls?
- How often does the board review current financial information?
- Has the organization obtained audited financials from an outside auditor?
- Have auditors noted any concerns, and have they been addressed?
- Does trust lead to weak internal controls and an absence of accountability?

We should be cautious about reaching conclusions based solely on one year's financial information. An organization's use of financial resources and ability to raise funds may vary from year to year, depending on its plans and other factors. For instance, a small organization with a bold strategic plan may commit a greater percentage of its financial resources to fundraising in a given year or two in order to meet its goals. An organization may need additional staff or expertise to expand or improve in performance. If you have concerns, discuss them with the organization's leaders to understand better what led to the numbers.

A Clear Mission Focus

What is the mission of the ministry? What need is the ministry seeking to meet?

An organization's articles of incorporation state its purpose. These can usually be found online through the office of the Secretary of State in the state of incorporation. The broader the description of an organization's purpose, the greater the opportunity for it to experience mission drift or mission dilution. Some ministries have more than one area of service, such as seeking to address education, housing, health, and job training. Is the organization equipped to be effective in multiple activities? Is it attempting to do too much in light of its resources? If so, it may be mediocre in meeting many needs rather than excellent in meeting one need. Organizations may be tempted to expand their mission to meet additional needs, rather than seeking to work with another ministry to address those needs.

Is the organization staying true to its mission? Though every organization should have a written mission statement, some ministries are pulled from their God-given mission because they need donations. The influence of large donors can be contrary to the mission.

In *Mission Drift*, Peter Greer, president of HOPE International, describes another way that mission drift can occur.[2] A few years ago, a corporation offered to provide a very large donation to HOPE if Peter would agree to diminish HOPE's emphasis on evangelism.

This made him aware of the power of money to pull a ministry off course. He could have rationalized accepting the offer by seeing the strings attached to the donation as "God's direction" for HOPE. But he and the board of HOPE discussed this and decided to walk away from the offer and remain true to the mission.

Assessment of Impacts

Good ideas for ministry don't guarantee results. In addition, some methods of ministry are more effective than others. For example, one of the most promising ideas for fighting malaria was providing bed nets to those at risk for mosquito bites. In the beginning, it was assumed those given the nets would use them when sleeping. But the nets had a more immediate purpose to those who received them—one study showed that some recipients chose to use the nets for fishing.[3] Various changes were made to address the attraction of alternative uses, depending on the location and need.

What evidence tells leaders that the activities of the ministry lead to accomplishing its *mission?* Good organizations develop methods to measure impact. For instance, if an organization seeks to improve the reading ability of elementary-age children, information on increasing numbers of children in a reading program does *not* reveal the program's impact. The desired impact is improved reading ability, not participation in the reading program. What testing or other means have they used to determine the impact on reading ability, and what were the results of the testing?

Also ask whether studies are available from other sources that report on the effectiveness of a type of ministry activity. Many universities and other organizations conduct studies on the effectiveness of such groups.[4] For instance, *Christianity Today* recently highlighted the positive results of an economist's study of Compassion International's child support program.[5] Good leadership of an organization should know about relevant studies.

Conflicts of Interest

A conflict of interest exists when a decision maker (or family member) personally benefits from a decision being made. For example, the ministry may contract with a board member's business for goods or services. In these situations, the board member should not be part of any decision-making on the transactions with his or her business or family. The board of directors should approve any arrangement involving a conflict without the conflicted party voting. A board-approved conflict of interest policy should define *conflict* and how the board is to address one.

Here are other questions regarding leadership you might ask:

- What are the longer-term needs of those served? (For example, how is a ministry educating children where few job opportunities exist?)

- How is the ministry working in partnership with the local church?

- What disappointments and problems have they encountered? What did they learn from these?

- Does the organization work toward excellence? Is it seeking to improve continuously to the glory of God? Or is grace an excuse for mediocrity?

- Is expansion more important than excellence?

- Is the ministry a praying and learning organization?

- Does the ministry give thanks to and praise God internally and externally?

- Does the ministry encourage and support everyone's use of his or her gifts for the kingdom of God, regardless of gender or ethnicity?

And don't forget this question: Where does the ministry see the Holy Spirit at work in its activities? What has happened in the ministry that clearly was of God, because human effort was or would have been insufficient?

This discussion on evaluating an organization is not intended to be exhaustive. And depending on the size of our donation, many questions may not be needed.

PART 3

Meeting
the Challenges
Along the Way

CHAPTER 10

Challenge to Generosity 1

Fear

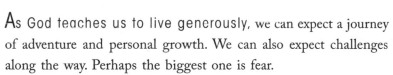

As God teaches us to live generously, we can expect a journey of adventure and personal growth. We can also expect challenges along the way. Perhaps the biggest one is fear.

In 2005, Hurricane Rita raced toward the Galveston Bay Area in Texas. Up the ship channel sat Houston. It was predicted that only the southern part of the Houston area would be impacted by life-threatening floodwaters from the tidal surge. As Hurricane Rita bore down on the coast, those living in Galveston and the southern part of Houston began to evacuate at the local government's request.

However, the evacuation planners didn't consider that individuals living in the northern parts of Houston would choose to evacuate as well, and everyone had to use the same routes out. Most of Houston was not in danger of life-threatening flooding or winds, yet an estimated 2.5 to 3.7 million people fled.[1] Gridlock ensued, and vehicles ran out of gasoline. Tragically, more people died trying to escape than from the effects of the storm. Why did Houstonians not in harm's way choose to leave? Fear.

Why such strong fear? Just three weeks before, Hurricane Katrina had struck New Orleans, a few hundred miles up the Gulf Coast. Stories and photos of suffering and anarchy had shocked us all. Fear interfered with reasonable decision making and blinded people to the very real dangers in evacuating.

Fear is a powerful motivator. And it's a part of being human—a God-given protective mechanism. But if fear is the most powerful influence on our decisions, it becomes *the* authority in our lives. Fear may highlight valid considerations in making wise decisions, but it should not determine our choices. Yet, for many of us, security for our families and ourselves is *the* highest priority. We sometimes deny this and label the resulting fear-driven self-protection as "wisdom."

In *Following Jesus in a Culture of Fear*, Scott Bader-Saye addressed how fear can lead us to make cowardly—sometimes stupid—decisions:

> When our moral lives are shaped by fear, and safety is worshiped as the highest good, we are tempted to make health and security the primary justifications for right action. We thus lead timid lives, fearing the risks of bold gestures. Instead of being courageous, we are content to be safe. Instead of being hopeful, we make virtues of cynicism and irony, which in turn keep us a safe distance from risky commitments. We are more likely to tell our children to "be careful" than to "be good." The extravagant vision that would change the world gets traded in for the passive axiom "do no harm."[2]

Our discipleship is starving on this "diet of self-protection."[3] And so is our generosity.

Most of us remember the significance of September 11, 2001. Another date, December 11, 2008,[4] is one on which Americans suffered greatly. Households lost $6.9 trillion as the result of the stock market's drastic drop.[5]

Bad things can happen financially that we can't predict or prevent. Will our businesses suffer a decline? Will our investments retain their value? Will Social Security and Medicare or my company's pension provide a safety net for me when I can't work any longer? Will I have medical insurance? Have we saved enough not to be a burden to our children?

We wonder, will we have enough? One of Americans' greatest concerns is that they will run out of money before their lives come to an end.[6]

We know that we can't save our way to security. So we face fundamental questions: Do we trust God to take care of us? Do we believe that God loves us? We can say yes yet make decisions in response to fear. We know that love is not the same as trust. Life experiences may have taught us that someone can love us and not be trustworthy. As a consequence, we may wonder if we can trust God to care for our families. We make ourselves a promise—mostly subconsciously—that we are going to do everything we can to take care of our families and ourselves.

Yet God assures us he does love us, is trustworthy, and is with us in all circumstances. He is good. He is *for us*. He invites us to trust him even when we don't understand. Ironically, we trust things we don't understand regularly—vaccinations, microwave ovens, smartphones, the Internet, the Cloud—and we nonchalantly put our lives on the line in aluminum tubes that fly forty-five thousand feet up. Why are we sometimes willing to believe that the news media delivers more truth than God's promises?

Money is the number-one source of security for most people, even many Christians. As a friend at church said, "I don't want to be rich. I just want enough that I don't have to depend on God." So sharing time and talent is much easier than giving money.

We may be tempted to trust investments, economic policies, the advice of others, and our own experience rather than our God who runs the universe. In an effort to protect our families and ourselves, we store up more than we need and then add a bit more, just in case. We describe such behavior as "wisdom," pointing to the uncertainty of the world we live in. In doing this, we have the illusion that we can provide for our needs and protect those we love.

Jesus told a story about a man who saved out of fear. In the parable of the bags of gold, the master leaves different amounts of money with each of three servants (Matthew 25:14-30). Two invest and make money for the master, but one does not. He buries the money in the dirt. When the master returns, he is pleased with the first two servants and says, "Well done, good and faithful servant!" (Matthew 25:21). The third servant, however, is severely reprimanded and thrown out. His fear had led him to do nothing but protect against loss. Yet the money entrusted to him was not a resource to do with as he pleased. It belonged to the master. And the master had expectations.

That third servant didn't spend the money improperly or selfishly. Rather, he simply did nothing. The master reprimands the servant, who had such a low opinion of his master. If we fear God is an unmerciful taskmaster, we act like the servant, saving our resources in a place we believe to be secure.

When I was a child, my parents gave my brother and me each a quarter to slip into the offering envelope for Sunday school. I always placed the envelope in the offering plate without any concern about there being more in the future. I trusted my parents to meet my needs, so I gave with freedom. In the same way, our heavenly Father seeks to demonstrate that he can be trusted to care for us. He is a bottomless resource for meeting our needs.

Fear constricts the heart, stifles our joy, and smothers our freedom.

In Luke 21:1-4, we read Jesus' observation of a poor widow who gives two small coins as a temple offering, a pittance compared to the gifts of the richer individuals. Jesus chose this opportunity to teach his followers why she gave more than the others. Her giving reveals her heart—not only her faithfulness to God, but also her belief that God is faithful to her as well. This story is a story of her *total surrender and trust, not so much of her sacrificial giving.*

We might give "sacrificially" without full surrender to God. We might decide to give sacrificially because we are motivated by the praise of others or the need for self-esteem. Jesus saw the widow's heart and saw a heart fully trusting in God.

In God's walk with his people throughout history, he never leads them to independence but to growing dependence. Our biblical heroes and heroines were very dependent on God. For example, a small band of twelve apostles and other disciples carried the message of Jesus to the other nations amid great opposition (and with no New Testament—or hymnal). His plan entailed their full surrender and dependence, and it has not changed.

Fear is a fact of life on earth. So how can we become fear's master rather than fear being our master?

Remember God's Faithfulness

Scripture encourages us to *remember* (for example, see 1 Chronicles 16:12). One of the benefits of keeping a journal, particularly a prayer journal, is seeing how God has been faithful to provide for us in the past.

Lynne is a professional with three children, one of whom is in college. A few years ago, her marriage ended. After the divorce settlement, she was left with the debt from her ex-husband's failed business. With God's guidance, she courageously developed a plan to pay off the debt as well as the college expenses of her children. She could easily have justified postponing her giving, but she didn't.

Lynne gave when she became aware of a need, even though it meant sacrificing something in her constrained budget. She explained her decisions simply: "God has always, always, *always* been faithful. He will be again."

Taking the Next Step, Regardless

With each step in faith, our faith grows.

Taking the next step is faith in action. Fear's grip on us lessens with each step we take. Eradicating fear is not the litmus test of whether we are living faithfully. The test is what we *do* in the face of fear. The best way to be courageous is simply to do the next thing, to take the next step on the journey.

With each giving decision, you may face fear. I confess that I do each year when I plan my giving. I ask, why not wait until I'm more certain I have enough for the future or when I die? We have to remember that when we face this fear, we've been around that mountain before. Take a deep breath, and keep going. It's like hiking up a mountain; each trip around the mountain is a shorter trip.

Fear is the number-one obstacle to living generously. The good news is that God knows us even better than we know ourselves. He can take honest admissions of fear and uncertainty when we ask to trust him more. He longs to show us the breadth and depth of his love *and* his trustworthiness.

Fear can be a powerful obstacle. But it is not the only obstacle we may face.

CHAPTER 11

Challenge to Generosity 2

A Desire for More

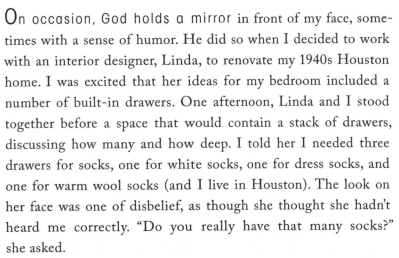

On occasion, God holds a mirror in front of my face, some-times with a sense of humor. He did so when I decided to work with an interior designer, Linda, to renovate my 1940s Houston home. I was excited that her ideas for my bedroom included a number of built-in drawers. One afternoon, Linda and I stood together before a space that would contain a stack of drawers, discussing how many and how deep. I told her I needed three drawers for socks, one for white socks, one for dress socks, and one for warm wool socks (and I live in Houston). The look on her face was one of disbelief, as though she thought she hadn't heard me correctly. "Do you really have that many socks?" she asked.

If I died today, family and friends would have questions about my three drawers of socks: Why did she buy so many socks? Did she think there was going to be a run on socks? Was she going to grow more feet? Did she think socks get better if stored and aged? And I had to ask, "Why *do* I have so many socks?"

Spending is not bad. God provides resources to care for our families and to bless others, too. In fact, it can be unwise not to spend. Think of the potential consequences of neglecting to purchase new tires, new air filters, and new underwear. But every dollar spent is a dollar that can't be given.

Does our culture encourage spending? Yes, powerfully. Americans bought items totaling $10.7 trillion when shopping in 2011.[1] In that same year, we spent $1.4 billion on teeth whiteners, $500 million on golf balls, $800 million on taxidermy (hmm), and $65 billion on soft drinks.[2] That year we also paid $10 billion for romance novels and $4.2 billion for perfume.[3] We spent approximately $7 billion on Halloween in 2015[4] and $350 million on Halloween costumes—for our *pets*.[5]

We are not alone. Other countries in the West also spend quite a bit. United Kingdom golfers spent £4.3 billion in 2014 on golf.[6] In 2013, Canada led the way in spending on makeup, spending Can$1.4 billion.[7] (Other countries have missed the Halloween pet costume trend, however. Please don't tell them.)

How much stuff do we have? So much that we don't have anywhere to store it. As a consequence, the offsite storage business is booming. We used to use closets for our storage. Then we parked the car in the driveway and began to use our garages. If that wasn't quite enough storage space, we bought a small tin house with squeaky metal doors for the backyard. Today we rent offsite storage space. (No squeaky doors.)

The declutter movement soon followed. If we don't know how to store all our stuff, we can turn to a book or a blog that tells us how to get rid of it.

How *did* we end up with so much stuff?

When we dig deep into our motivations, we often find places in our hearts that need healing. Do I want to make my home welcoming and comfortable, or do I want to impress my visitors? Do I own certain possessions, dress a certain way, and participate in certain activities because I want to fit in with a certain group? Do we have the same desires for our children—hoping they feel like they fit in? All of these questions originate from a concern about what others think of us.

Desire to Belong

Have you ever walked into a room of people at an event and said to yourself, *I don't have the right clothes on for this?* I have. (Is this just a female thing?) When I joined the YMCA a few years ago, I showed up in sweatpants and an old T-shirt. To my surprise, the women were wearing matching spandex tops and pants and matching socks and hair clasps. (The men were wearing shorts that looked like they were purchased in college and T-shirts bought on last year's vacation.) What did I do? I cut my exercise routine short and left before someone I knew showed up.

We're tempted to allow our contentment to be determined by how well we measure up when we compare ourselves with others. As we see others with the newest homes, clothes, cars, and electronics, we are tempted to grow dissatisfied with what we have. For most of us, our social discontent stems less from envy than from a desire to fit in.

In 1992 I needed a new car. Because my Maxima had been reliable, I bought a new Maxima. Reliability and cost were my only considerations. After an automobile accident ten years later, I needed another car. Another Maxima? Not this time.

Although I began with researching the safest car, I was influenced by my peers at work, who drove BMWs, Volvos, and Lexuses (Lexi?). When I attended company events, I saw that other managers didn't drive Maximas. So I bought a BMW. I have to admit I enjoyed driving it. And I felt safer. And I felt better about parking it in the managers' parking lot with the other managers. (I didn't realize that a pickup truck would also fit in. This is Texas.) So I fit in when the restaurant valet delivered the cars after company functions. I didn't want to make an impression; I just wanted to fit in.

Desire for Beauty

Beauty, they say, is in the eye of the beholder. Claude Monet's painting of water lilies entitled *Nymphéas* sold for $54 million at a Sotheby's auction in 2014.[8] A pink designer purse sold for £150,000 at a Christie's auction in Hong Kong.[9] The CCXR Trevita is the most expensive car in the world—even more than a Ferrari—costing close to $5 million.[10] All three of these are beautiful in the eyes of their owners.

We are made to enjoy beauty. God endowed us each with an appreciation for it—simply based on how something looks or sounds. He planted love of beauty in our hearts.

We can easily let an appreciation for beauty develop into a desire to own it. A friend and I were looking at purses in a department store when she found a red one she admired. Her eyes twinkled. When I encouraged her to buy it, she said no as she put it back on the shelf. I thought her concern was cost. Instead, she said, "I'm learning to enjoy beauty without having to own it." Hmm. There's an interesting thought. Can we appreciate beautiful things without seeking to own them?

Desire for Comfort and Convenience

Easy, quick, comfortable, and convenient. These are some of our values. We are busy. Our time is limited. We are in a hurry. So we spend for these reasons too.

How many times have I walked into a Target to get one thing and left with ten others, thinking, *As long as I'm here, I should pick up* . . . I'm convinced this is how I ended up with three drawers of socks. It was just convenient.

The desire for comfort and convenience has led to television remotes, microwaves, drive-through pharmacies and cleaners, and home delivery with setup of most anything. Ironically, we buy gadgets to wear to encourage us to move, because these other purchases lead to less movement.

Today most of us have several televisions. Julie and Sam, friends of mine down the street, have only one television. Julie called to have her cable connection restored after a storm. The young cable service representative answering the phone asked how many televisions she had in the home. "One," Julie said.

Silence. Then, "You have only one television? I have never received a call from someone who had only one television."

Julie's family had learned to be content with one.

You may be familiar with the apostle Paul's description of the various circumstances in which he lived. He said he had *learned* to be content in all situations. He then explained how he did so: "I can do all things through him who strengthens me" (Philippians 4:13 NRSV). Yes, that well-known second verse is in reference to *contentment.* Paul had *learned* to be content, not by his strength, but by the strength Christ gave him. We can learn to be content in the same way.

Desire for Affirmation

The world tells us money is a sign of worth and success. With it comes privilege and power. We know our identity is in Christ, but living as though that's true calls us not to measure our worth according to the world.

The things we purchase can provide a sense of gratification or self-esteem, even if temporarily. Although the desire is natural, the nearest boutique, spa, or shopping mall isn't where desires are met.

We won't meet them in the corner office, the country club, or the stadium. God placed these desires in us, intending that we won't fulfill them except in him.

Women are subject to significant pressure to look attractive, beginning at an early age. In our Western culture, this means looking young and thin. What is one result of this cultural pressure? The United States is number one in spending on cosmetics.[11] And is anyone happy with the result? Not in bright lighting.

Our desires may be born out of pressure from others, often unintended. Does my husband still find me attractive? Are my children embarrassed by me or by our home? Will my children have to endure ridicule because they're viewed as "uncool" or "weird"?

Some of us spend as the result of an experience of rejection, abandonment, ridicule, or shame that left us feeling we weren't enough. Avoiding the pain of negative prior experiences is a powerful driver for our decisions.

Experiences that make us feel we aren't enough can lead to vows to prove otherwise or to avoid feeling that painful emotion again.[12] We use money on what "our crowd" or our desired crowd does, whether it's the car we drive, the neighborhood we live in, or the clothes we wear.

We believe that if we *have* enough, we will *be* enough.

Desire for Happiness

Our emotions can have a powerful impact on how we choose to use money. Spending is where some of us turn when we experience painful emotions, such as loneliness, boredom, grief, anger, and rejection. There is even a term for this: retail therapy.[13] Is our purchasing a distraction, an escape, or an activity that makes us feel happy?

In 2014, Americans spent more than $70 billion on lottery tickets—more than on sports, movies, music, video games, and books combined.[14] We wouldn't be playing the lottery if we didn't believe more money would make us happier. Yet we regularly read stories of lottery winners who lose much more than their winnings—stories of robberies, murders, divorces, bankruptcy, and hounding relatives and friends.

The desire for money is like a bucket that's never full. More is always better. In a recent study, Michael Norton, a professor at Harvard Business School, surveyed people with at least $1 million. He asked how much would be enough to make their lives happy.[15] Regardless of how much money they made, they each believed that if they had three times more, they would reach the level guaranteeing happiness. Those with $1 million desired $3 million. Those with $3 million wanted $9 million. His conclusion: more money does not increase happiness. So, why do we believe it will? His conclusion: "One of the curses of being human is that we like to count things. It's hard to count how good your marriage is, but it's easy to count money, square footage and inches on a TV."[16]

Coffee, chocolate, and books make me happy. I don't spend much on chocolate. I do like good coffee. And please don't ask me what I spend on books. Although these aren't bad things, the happiness they offer is temporary. Of course, it's okay to purchase and enjoy things, but all good things have a cost. The *real* cost is that those funds might have been used for something more valuable.

The question for us is whether we're seeking God's guidance on our purchases. God desires to bless our families with good things. But are we living as though the only true and lasting source of joy is our relationship with God—or our stuff and what others think? Our Creator placed in us a yearning *only he* can satisfy. He designed us so we will seek our joy in him (which will last much longer than the smell of new shoes or a new car).

CHAPTER 12

Challenge to Generosity 3

Subconscious Beliefs

Our culture mounts great pressure on us to spend. Spending becomes as natural as tying our shoes. Often our decisions are made without recognizing the drivers in our lives that lead to these decisions, including subconscious beliefs about money and giving.

We Worked Hard for Our Money, So It's Ours

Sandy is a young MBA graduate in a prominent investment firm just beginning her career. She works the long hours new MBAs are expected to work on the path to becoming a partner in her firm. I joined her one afternoon for a cup of coffee and conversation.

The conversation soon turned to financial giving. Having had a negative experience with a nonprofit, she said it was difficult for her to give. Then she exclaimed, "I work hard for my money!" I understand her feelings. I had worked those long hours as a lawyer for many years.

We can easily believe we've earned everything that's ours. After all, we did work hard. We made sacrifices. We lived on Hamburger Helper and pot pies for years. We pulled all-nighters, drinking coffee to meet deadlines. And we held our car together with duct tape (if we had one). For years we paid off our college loan debt. We made good decisions, planning for the future. We earned our grades in school. We earned ours jobs and success. We earned our paychecks and promotions. So can't we do as we please with our financial resources, except for maybe giving to our local church? The rest is ours, right?

This isn't God's plan. When God gave to his chosen people, they were to possess his gifts as stewards, not as owners (Deuteronomy 3:18; 8:10-18; 11:29). As stewards, they were to be blessed, but also to bless to others. We use the word *ownership* today in our economic and legal systems, but God remains the true owner of everything. Even *we* belong to God (1 Corinthians 6:20; 7:23).

We also didn't earn our blessings. We didn't earn the country in which we live or our health, aptitude, skills, and opportunities. We didn't earn our families, teachers, and mentors. *Everything* has been given to us. We have a very generous God.

So, what are we to do with our blessings? Jesus told the story of a rich man whose crops produced more than he needed and more than his barns could hold. He faced a decision: what would he do with this excess? The rich man decided to save it by building bigger barns and taking it easy for the rest of his life. (Retirement?) That very night, however, God called him a fool. His life was coming to an end, and others would reap the benefits. Jesus ended the story with this point: "This is how it will be with whoever stores up things for themselves but is not rich toward God" (Luke 12:21).

This man was successful by the world's standards. And he wasn't intentionally harming others. He simply kept everything for his family without considering that God intended that he use it for the benefit of others.

Can We Save Too Much?

Renee had a successful medical practice as an obstetrician in the Austin area. Her success provided both professional and financial rewards. Though she had reached many of her goals, she felt something was missing.

One day while she was running in a park, Renee heard God tell her, "I want you to work like a doctor and live like a nurse." From that point forward, her financial decisions were part of a process of surrendering all of her life to God. Renee explains,

> After I paid off my student loans, I began saving heavily, maxing out my retirement account and investing in stocks and real estate—things most people would have viewed as responsible. But God had other ideas about how to distribute what he had so generously provided, and reminded me that my future was in his hands. . . . I realized my large salary could be used to improve the lives of others today, as I trust God to meet tomorrow's needs. So I stopped saving so much and started giving more generously.[1]

As her giving increased, God continued to provide for her. He developed in her a greater understanding and compassion for others who must live on a budget. And she now feels free of the need to be understood or approved by others. She thinks of her life change as deciding to "live wholeheartedly."

When asked what she would say to those who want to make a similar change, Renee shared the following advice:

- Take a mission trip. Notice the joy in the simpler lifestyles as well as the interdependence of those in the community you serve.

- Schedule times of solitude to listen to God. Ask, am I surrendered? In what ways am I not living wholeheartedly toward God?

- Be accountable financially to others, such as friends and a financial adviser.

Our Giving Won't Do Much Good

Many of the world's greatest needs can be traced to poverty: poor health, lack of education, human trafficking, violence, addiction, government corruption, and a lack of opportunity to work. Poverty has been a long-term problem in the world.

To be honest, we can grow skeptical or even cynical about efforts to help the poor. The problem is too big. Previous efforts seemed to have failed. I admit that I was having a problem trusting God to accomplish his purposes. I experienced—and still experience—frustration, not fully understanding what God is doing. I've had to accept that giving is another step of faithfulness that leads me into the unknown—and to humility.

On a weeklong church mission trip, I worked alongside a ministry that had a rich history in the community. Witnessing the poverty there, I wondered what this ministry had accomplished. Why were the people still poor? The ministry had helped countless young people, the leaders explained, but they left for education opportunities and rarely returned. They wanted to raise their families in better homes and better neighborhoods. I realized I couldn't see the many individuals the ministry had impacted.

We who don't live in poverty, particularly in the West, can view ourselves as able—and even called—to decide what is best for others, particularly those living in financial poverty. In addition, we can expect positive results in a short period without recognizing that transformation is not a quick process.

Ending extreme poverty is possible.[2] Extreme poverty (defined as living on less than two dollars a day) is in retreat,[3] having been *cut in half* in thirty years.[4] Let's not pass by that last statement too quickly.

Progress has been made in medicine, education, water sanitation, agriculture, communication, technology, and many other areas. Modern vaccines, job creation, and technology have reduced health threats and poverty more than we have ever seen in history.

Have we failed to consider that God might be answering our prayers for the poor? We serve a mighty God who is active and involved in the world. For the first time in human history, we have the realistic possibility of seeing the end of extreme global poverty— not just someday, but in our lifetime.[5]

What do we really know about the needs in the world? Before we reach conclusions, we might consider seeking to learn more. Talking with those serving has helped me understand better, rather than applying assumptions based on my experience alone. Education is also available at universities and online. We owe it to ourselves (and others?) to find out just what the status of a need is in the world today.

We Know More About Solving Problems Than They Do

Discussions about the West's efforts to help resulting in harm have been going on for decades. For various reasons, we in the West assume we know how to solve others' problems. Sometimes these assumptions involve the value we place on institutional education. But all knowledge, creativity, and vision do not reside solely with us.

We move forward to solve problems because of compassion and with a can-do attitude. We sincerely want to help, and we're sure we can. But in doing this, we may do more harm than good. In the documentary film *Poverty, Inc.*,[6] one of the producers maintains that the traditional way of giving fails in the worst way. He shared this example:

A Rwandan egg farmer who was just getting his business started when a well-meaning American church decided to send free eggs to his starving countrymen. Overnight, the local entrepreneur found himself unable to sell his own goods in the market. Although locals benefited for a short time, when the church turned its philanthropic attention elsewhere, it had driven the farmer out of business and inadvertently crippled the local egg economy.[7]

Even with good intentions, have we become part of the problem? When immediate basic needs need to be met temporarily, relief organizations need to quickly do more to support local citizens in their efforts to solve local problems.

I Shouldn't Give Unless I'm Certain in My Giving Decisions

Ann wondered if she and her husband, John, had made a wise decision. They share a passion for ending oppression and genocide, and the investment firm they founded and its charitable foundation chose to contribute to efforts to track down Joseph Kony, the head of the Lord's Resistance Army (LRA). The LRA massacred unimaginable numbers of people in Uganda, the Central African Republic, South Sudan, and the Democratic Republic of Congo.[8] This army included kidnapped children, who—trained as child soldiers—were taught to kill their own families and others. The government's military in Uganda, with the help of US military advisers, had been seeking to catch the notorious warlord for many years.

The charitable foundation and other partner organizations learned the Ugandan soldiers needed additional training to resist the LRA, so they focused on supporting the training of soldiers. In addition, the Ugandan army needed a critical piece of equipment to increase effectiveness: a helicopter. The group provided funds. With the aid of the helicopter, the Ugandan army was able to track down the LRA. Today the LRA's effectiveness has largely been destroyed.

Ann said that at the time of the decision, she wondered whether they gave wisely. After all, she and John could have given those dollars to a well-established organization like International Justice Mission. When she reflected on their decision, she pointed out, "Courage is required to give. You may wonder if you have made the right decision. There will always be other seemingly good alternatives. But one has to step out in faith."[9]

Giving requires *two* steps of faith. The first is deciding to give. (We all know letting go of money is a step of faith.) The second is deciding who to give to. Although we can research giving opportunities, we can never be completely confident that our donation will be used for good for maximum impact. If we wait for that moment of 100 percent certainty, we don't give generously.

I would like to be 100 percent certain of my giving decisions. I would like God to write the number in the sky or use a coin toss. But sometimes what motivates me is an underlying desire to be *right* in my giving decisions, not a desire to grow in my relationship with God. What am I afraid of?

God clearly wants to include us as participants in his plans. He invites us to be his coworkers (1 Corinthians 3:9). God wants to share the joy of giving, and he wants us to grow in our trust of him. He wants to develop in us a heart like Jesus' and deepen our relationship with others. When we understand why God has invited us to be involved with him in the world, we see that the idea he might toss a dollar amount at us or write an organization's name in the sky is clearly unrealistic.

As we work, God also works in us. The Holy Spirit transforms our hearts to be more like God's heart for the world. He desires that we grow in character and closeness to him more than that we make the "right" decision.

These unrecognized beliefs, as well as others, may influence our giving. Often they bring emotional reactions. For our giving to be generous and wise, we need to be thoughtful and prayerful.

CHAPTER 13

Challenge to Generosity 4

Not Making a Plan

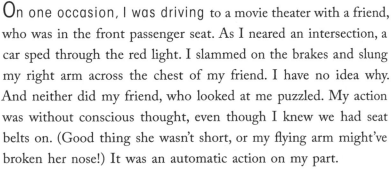

On one occasion, I was driving to a movie theater with a friend, who was in the front passenger seat. As I neared an intersection, a car sped through the red light. I slammed on the brakes and slung my right arm across the chest of my friend. I have no idea why. And neither did my friend, who looked at me puzzled. My action was without conscious thought, even though I knew we had seat belts on. (Good thing she wasn't short, or my flying arm might've broken her nose!) It was an automatic action on my part.

Reasoned decision making is not the basis for all our behavior. All of us have long-ingrained habits of which we aren't fully aware.[1] Our brains take a time-out, like when the alarm goes off in the morning and initiates our morning routine: taking vitamins, putting on exercise clothes, turning on the coffee pot, and unplugging electronic devices from chargers. We don't think much about doing these activities. We just do them out of habit.

Scientists tell us that about 40 percent of the decisions we make every day are made unintentionally as the result of habits we have developed.[2] Because we make more decisions each day than our brain can process, our brain looks for shortcuts to reduce the energy required for decision making.

A decision to save or spend may be the result of habit. Although we may want to be generous, we have a default mindset that operates when we make financial decisions. For most of us, giving isn't our default mindset; it's spending or saving. As a consequence, we must be intentional about giving. We have to override our default.

Making an annual plan helps us to be intentional. Some of us naturally like to make plans. We spend an hour looking at new calendars at the beginning of a new year. We value schedules, reservations, maps, and preprinted to-do list pads.

For others, our idea of a plan is deciding the next step—just in time. In reality, we all plan, if only in the creation of to-do lists. At my house, if a task is not on the to-do list, it's not going to get done.

We all need a plan for our giving.

Getting Started

A giving plan is a simple document on which we set our giving goals. Our plan helps us to give wisely and be diligent in our giving. The format can be any one that works for you. (I have included an example of an annual giving plan in appendix E.)

Begin by setting a goal for the year. How much do you want to give in total during the year? Then list the organizations you plan to give to during the year and the amount you'll give to each.

Also consider including the amounts you gave during the previous year, as a reference when setting the amount to be given in the current year. Looking back at your giving allows you to reflect on your progress in growing in generosity.

Note on your plan the organizations you need to reevaluate because of the time that has passed since your last review. Check to see if any changes have occurred in the ministry during the year, such as its mission, leadership, or financial stability. If you increase your giving, consider taking a deeper look at the organization than previously. You may also want to do so if new information raises questions.

God is full of surprises on the giving journey. In your list of recipients, include a category labeled "Miscellaneous" or "Holy Spirit's Surprise." This line item is a placeholder amount for opportunities the Holy Spirit brings before you during the year. These opportunities may include anything from disaster relief to a solicitation from a neighbor's child. (Though buying Girl Scout cookies doesn't count unless we give the cookies away.)

Your giving plan also can be used to plan for the giving of your time and skills. Also consider including goals for giving during your projected lifespan. In doing so, you can plan to do most of your giving during your lifetime and when you're healthy. Such a plan can be adjusted annually for changes in circumstances or information.

Your giving plan isn't a set of inflexible limits on your giving. As the writer of Proverbs wrote, "We can make our plans, but the Lord determines our steps" (Proverbs 16:9 NLT). Your plan serves as a tool to ensure you are intentional and faithful in your giving.

Allocating Annual Giving Among Many Giving Opportunities

To maximize the impact of their gift, donors often concentrate their giving on a few organizations. Giving to only a few organizations can help us focus our giving and limit our due diligence (and the emails in the inbox). If you give substantially to an organization, the ministry's leaders may view you as part of a group of strategic partners.

Another allocation method is to divide our giving among ministries that serve in one of the ways Jesus did, such as making disciples, giving to the poor, caring for the widow and orphan, visiting the prisoner, freeing the oppressed, and caring for our neighbor (Isaiah 42:7; Luke 4:17-19).

Another method is to consider allocating our annual giving amount in a manner similar to an investment portfolio. In an investment portfolio, the total amount invested is typically divided among investments of different risk. If we want to minimize the risk of our investments, we can choose investments less likely to lose value, even though those investments generally won't carn as much. With the help of a financial adviser, we allocate investment dollars based on the potential reward and the risk of loss.

So take a similar approach when allocating your giving dollars. For instance, give a certain percentage to an established, rock-solid ministry. At the other end of the spectrum, allocate a certain percentage to a promising startup organization. Such an organization has a higher risk of failing than the well-established ministry, but support is needed for those addressing unaddressed needs or testing new ideas, or working in new geographical areas.

Here's another allocation consideration: we might give a percentage to ministries that focus on emergency relief after natural disasters—such as hurricanes, earthquakes, and droughts—while contributing another percentage to ministries addressing circumstances that contribute to disasters. Our hearts may prompt us to take action, but giving to relief organizations also should be done thoughtfully. We should do our due diligence on organizations we consider, and give only to credible ones. It's not usually a good idea to give to someone soliciting on the phone after one of these events.

Prevention-oriented organizations focus on such needs as hygiene, clean water, preventive health care, agriculture practices, business development, safe structures, and education. Some donors describe giving to prevention-oriented organizations as a way to address the *root causes* of a problem, rather than addressing the results of a problem. An example is contributing toward bed nets for protection against mosquitoes, rather than for medical treatment for malaria.

Giving to organizations seeking to solve systemic problems will likely have the broadest impact, but the impact may take longer to develop. Sometimes we can't address deeper causes, such as war. Nevertheless, we may want to consider supporting a ministry that serves victims, even though it doesn't provide a permanent solution to the underlying problem. An example is giving to a ministry that serves refugees from a war-torn country.

We might also consider allocating our total giving among local ministries, ministries in the United States, and international ministries. Prayerfully consider giving to needs beyond your own backyard. According to Giving USA, in 2010 Americans gave only 5 percent of their giving outside of the United States.[3] Americans might be forgetting the needs of the majority of the world.

Launch a Giving Fund Using a Donor-Advised Fund

Amazingly, many donors aren't familiar with a Donor-Advised Fund (DAF). This is a mystery to me. Setting up one saves time, effort, and money. And who doesn't want to save more of these? You can set up one up with National Christian Foundation (NCF, national christian.com) or WaterStone (waterstone.org), or many major mutual funds. Think of a DAF account as your giving fund.

Here's how it works. You contribute money, stock, and mutual fund interests to a DAF. If the DAF is National Christian Foundation, you can also contribute to business interests, real estate, and even the farm Grandma gave you. At the time you make this gift to the DAF, you have a federal tax-deductible charitable donation in the amount of the *current* value of what was donated.

For example, you contribute shares of stock that have increased in value, say from twenty dollars at the time of purchase to one hundred. The amount of the charitable contribution is the value of the stock when given to the DAF (one hundred dollars). If you sold the stock, you would have to pay federal income taxes on the profit from the sale (one hundred dollars minus twenty equals a profit of eighty dollars). The result is a smaller gift (what's left after you pay taxes from the sale). If you give the stock to the DAF, they sell the stock. Then you don't have to pay federal income taxes, you have a tax-deductible contribution, and the ministry receives more.

Also consider accelerating your giving into the DAF to maximize your charitable deduction from federal income taxes during your high-income years, such as prior to retirement. After making large donations to your DAF, you can plan your giving over many years, taking the requisite time to make wise decisions about who will receive a gift out of the DAF.

Another advantage to using a DAF is the convenience. All your giving can be done online; DAF handles sending checks. Most DAFs provide the option to set up recurring payments to ministries, such as a monthly gift to a church.

My favorite convenience? Less paperwork. When we use a DAF, we receive *one* charitable contribution receipt for the preparation of our federal income tax return, so I retired my shoebox of charitable giving receipts. No more tracking down missing receipts when the tax adviser needs them for my tax return. (I now use the empty shoeboxes for other filing needs.)

A psychological benefit to using a DAF as our giving fund, rather than as a checking or savings account, is that once we donate into our giving fund at the DAF, the money is no longer accessible for any other use. Once the money is no longer in my hands, it's much easier to act to send money to ministries.

I'm not qualified to give tax advice, so I encourage you to contact a Christian professional tax adviser to discuss charitable giving plans. I hope the above discussion makes the point that obtaining tax advice on giving and starting a DAF account are both wise steps.

When Should I Give?

Our timing often affects the impact of decisions. History is replete with examples of bad timing. *Smart Money* magazine's October 2008 issue encouraged investing in the stock market, with the cover stating, "Double Your Nest Egg."[4] It was published on September 16, 2008, the day the stock market started dropping more than any time since the Great Depression. Another, Silverstein Properties in New York City, executed a ninety-nine-year lease on the Twin Towers of the World Trade Center on July 24, 2001, less than two months before 9/11.[5]

So, how should you time your gifts to ministries? A majority of giving from individuals occurs near the end of the year, after they know their tax status for the year. Unfortunately, this approach can leave ministries in need of support during the remainder of the year. Most ministries welcome an annual gift given proportionately on a twelve-month or quarterly schedule so that funds are received throughout the year. In addition, ministries experience a slowdown of gifts during the summer because of the distraction of summer activities. Keep these timing considerations in mind to support the smooth running of a ministry (and avoid causing insomnia for ministry leaders). A qualified tax adviser can help with estimating a certain amount you can give confidently.

An organization may seek a single large donation to expand operations, increase sustainability, or support a special project. Is it wise to give such a large donation? Consider whether your large gift will prompt an unwise immediate spending spree. Will the organization use the money prudently? Will the use of the money spur growth that's sustainable in the future? Are the leaders experienced in handling large one-time donations? Growth that shrinks when a gift is gone can wreck a ministry and hurt many.

We may be asked to contribute large donations to build facilities, begin new programs, or fund endowments. Before giving to these initiatives, consider these questions:

- Is the purpose of the project, program, or endowment clearly stated? Is it agreed in writing that the donation will be used only for the stated purpose?

- How will the organization provide for the cost of operation and the maintenance of the facility or program?

- Has the organization obtained the permits needed for the project?

- Does the organization own the land on which the facility will be built?

- Have local residents and community leaders been involved in the plans for the new facility or program?

- Are capable and reputable local contractors available for the project or program?

- Are local employees or specialists available to conduct operations?

- When will funds for the endowment be used, and how will the funds be managed in the interim?

(Additional resources on giving wisely can be found in appendix A.)

A giving plan is a necessary tool for giving effectively and consistently with God's direction. Without a plan, we are vulnerable to neglecting our giving as the result of busyness or emotional issues associated with money. We should hold our plan loosely though. God has the final plan.

CHAPTER 14

Donor Precautions

Using Influence

Seeking to determine whether an organization is well run and making an impact is reasonable, and we should expect transparency and candor. But we need to be mindful of the power that comes with a donation—particularly a large one. We can offer opinions, but the organization's leaders make the decisions. We may hold the ministry accountable for results, but we shouldn't seek to control it. If we are called to make decisions or lead, we should offer to volunteer and serve in leadership.

An Invitation to Serve on the Board of Directors

If you give regularly to an organization, the board of directors may invite you to join them as a member. Being part of a board is an effective way to serve in leadership and share opinions on the direction and strategy of the ministry. Often serving in this way is extremely rewarding and educational. You may have skills or experience from your business, employment, or volunteer activities that are helpful to the board's decision making.

Being on a board is a serious commitment. The board has fiduciary duties to the organization, similar to those of a trustee. They're responsible for the financial integrity and strategic direction of the ministry. Before agreeing to be on a board, you'll need to understand what you're signing up for. What are the expectations of board members? A good resource for those considering serving on a board is BoardSource (boardsource.org). And these questions may be helpful:

- What is the term of a member of the board, and what is the expectation of members in regard to attending meetings or participating on board committees?

- Ask, why was I asked to be a board member? How do they see you adding value to the current group in decision making, or are they just looking for another warm body?

- Who are the other board members, and how long have they served?

- What is the financial gift obligation of a board member? Part of a board member's commitment is a financial contribution, and they might have invited you mostly for this reason.

- In what ways do board members help with fundraising? In some organizations, particularly smaller ones, board members serve as the main development team. Or you may be asked to fill a table at a fundraiser or host a fundraising event in your home.

- What are the current problems or challenges the ministry is facing? You may be called to clean up a mess, chart a new direction, or find new leadership. Even so, you probably don't want to find this out *after* you agree to serve.

- Do any board members or officers have a conflict of interest with the organization?

- Do the latest strategic plan, financial reports, audits, and the current bylaws lead to further questions?

We Don't Know What We Don't Know

Kathy will never forget her first trip to the Dominican Republic to visit a ministry that provided medical treatment. The supervisor at a medical clinic took her on a tour of the clinic and explained that they were unable to serve many because the people lacked transportation to the clinic. Kathy was heartbroken, because it was apparent to her that an ambulance was needed to help transport those who were ill.

When she returned to the United States, she promptly made a contribution designated for purchasing an ambulance. She later learned from a board member and friend that the ambulance was not the greatest need of the ministry and that using an ambulance would be difficult because of congestion and potholes. Kathy then realized she didn't have enough information to make a gift designated for a specific purpose.

Many donors find it attractive to designate a gift for a specific purpose, such as for buildings, equipment, or technology. And nonprofit leaders recognize that donors are more likely to respond to appeals for a particular need. If a nonprofit requests a donation for an explicit purpose, be sure to specify in writing that the gift is for that purpose only.

Caution is warranted in designating a donation when the ministry leadership has not asked for funds for that purpose. We can't fully understand the needs and fluctuating circumstances of a ministry when we decide to restrict the use of our gift. Designating monies for a purpose may require other resources not available at the time of the gift. For example, designating monies for a particular piece of equipment is unwise if the organization lacks the personnel to operate it or the funds to maintain it.

Although we can share our opinions, it's best to avoid imposing our judgment on the ministry's priorities with the offer of a donation. Only the leadership is fully aware of all its needs and competing priorities.

It's best not to specify project deadlines or criticize the pace of a project's progress. The timeline to finish a project may need to be flexible. For example, local conditions may affect the availability of needed personnel, materials, and regulatory approvals.

It's wise to remember that funding day-to-day operations is almost every ministry's greatest need. We may be less excited about contributing to the operating expenses of a nonprofit, but support for operating expenses is critical to running a nonprofit. The utility bills have to be paid. Roofs have to be repaired. Those working for the ministry need to be paid a living wage to support their families.

Another necessary ministry cost is fundraising. To raise essential financial resources, ministry representatives engage with potential donors and invest time building relationships. Part of the responsibility of a ministry is to offer donors the opportunity to be faithful and to be part of God's work in the world.

Pride

An organization's leaders and staff will express gratitude but may also heap praise and recognition on us if we give a significant donation. We may receive photographs, crafts, personal notes, DVDs, books, or special gifts. They may invite us to sit at one of the front tables at fundraising events. We may be asked to more lunches than is good for our waistline. They may remember the name of our dog and ask about our mother. They will solicit our opinions and tell us how valuable we are to the organization—and they are quite sincere. But this can be heady stuff. Remember that we are merely the conduit of God's provision. We are simply God's servants, just like they are.

PART 4

Companions
on the Journey

CHAPTER 15

Giving with Family

As we consider money, we naturally begin to think about family. Before we decide to leave a sizable inheritance to our children, we should consider broadly what is in their best interest. Will they be blessed more by money for spending or saving, or by the deepening relationship with God and others that comes through giving as a family?

Leaving an Inheritance — a Blessing or a Danger?

My niece and nephew are precious to me. My refrigerator door is covered with their art. Thinking about the future, I decided to set up an account to assist them financially with their college education.

We want to care for our families after we die, so we should consider their needs as we plan for the disposition of our possessions and money. Leaving a large inheritance beyond their needs, however, may do more harm to them than good.

Two thirds of wealth transferred to heirs fails.[1] Parents may unintentionally neglect teaching their heirs how to handle the responsibility of money, and as a result, distrust and poor communication develop among the heirs.[2] One study concluded:

Many family leaders devoted far more time preparing their estate documents than they did to preparing their heirs for the impact of those documents. While the family leaders may have "learned by doing," the structure and complexity of the assets being handed down had grown substantially, and were no longer amenable to "learned stewardship on the fly."[3]

As we make estate-planning decisions, we should consider the potential negative consequences of bequeathing large sums of money to our children. What could the impact be on family values, family unity, character development, skill and talent development, and work ethic? Could a large inheritance lead to our heirs' increased anxiety or isolation, or make them vulnerable to the dishonesty or violence of others? Should our estate plan be mostly a giving plan?

If we have a surplus, we should take time to consider whether God's blessings placed in our hands are to be used for good during our lifetime, not after we're gone. Our part in God's mission in the world is not deferred until our death.

You may not need to sell the family home, an ongoing business, or other things that have sentimental value to your family. But consider how you can bless your family *and* give to God's work in the world now. You can't punt the responsibility to steward your resources to future generations when God has chosen you to do so. Could God be saying to you, "This opportunity is for you"?

If you're considering creating a charitable trust so your children can continue a family giving tradition, specify the types of charitable organizations or activities the trust gives to, so the gifts remain consistent with your values for future generations. Although your children and heirs may respect your values and wishes while you're alive, they may be influenced more strongly by others after you die. As Ron Blue says, "Do your givin' while you're livin,' so you're knowin' where it's goin.'"[4]

Why not develop a plan to do your major giving *during* your life with your family? Use the time together to teach your children gratitude for God's blessings and how to handle money. Show them how to make wise giving decisions as well as wise spending and saving decisions. You have an opportunity to introduce them to the world beyond their groups of friends and familiar places. Exposure to the needs in the world develops humility, compassion, gratitude, and wisdom. How else will they learn these?

Planning for family inheritances and giving during your lifetime requires the help of experts. A financial adviser and estate-planning attorney can both provide help in planning both giving during your lifetime and gifts to ministries at the time of your death.

Charitable giving can be any opportunity for the family to learn God's grace.

Reluctant Family Members

When we experience the beauty of a sunset or a fireworks display, we want to share such "wow" moments with those we love. As we experience the joy of generosity, we long to share that joy. For those who are married, there's no one we'd rather share this with than our spouse.

John and Ann married shortly after college. When John went to graduate school, Ann worked in the placement office at the school. When John graduated and started working, they looked forward to their first check so they could give. Later John formed his own business.

When John predicted the firm's financial success, he and Ann discussed the likely changes in their finances. What were they going to do with the increase in income? Ann said, "I had a house, two cars, one dog, and three children. What more did I want?" They decided then to limit their lifestyle. In addition, they committed 50 percent of the profits from the firm to the firm's charitable foundation.

Our family members, particularly spouses, may not be on the same page as we are on money matters. Often one spouse is a saver, and the other is a spender or a giver. When this is so, spouses aren't merely absent on the journey; they may become a drag on the journey. If that's your case, you may need patience.

A spouse may have anxiety about anything perceived as a threat to the security and well-being of the family. Many of us grew up in families that experienced a shortage of money, a failed business, or job loss—and the shame and fear that these can bring. This family experience influences our own thinking—and feelings—about money as adults.

Money is a heart matter, and only God can change the heart. So we can begin praying for our loved ones to gain a vision of God's generosity. Our goal is to encourage them in a manner that doesn't lead to guilt, but enables them to experience the joy of giving. We can affirm any steps of generosity and be patient with growth. It's a journey.

To encourage family members to give, invite them to generosity events where they will be with peers. Events with biblical teaching on giving can be enlightening. The events should provide a safe environment to consider the blessings and opportunities that come with money. What is a secure environment? One that isn't intimidating or guilt inducing. Joy should be at the heart of the message of living generously. Consider a Celebration of Generosity event[5] or a smaller event, like a Journey of Generosity.[6]

Jason attended his first Celebration of Generosity event after an invitation from a friend. Although the teaching and testimonies were powerful, the Holy Spirit used a little book to change his heart. At the book tables at the event, Jason chose a short book to read during a break, Randy Alcorn's *The Treasure Principle*.[7] Once he began reading, he couldn't stop. He then pulled out his Bible and began to look up every Bible verse referenced in the book. By the time he finished reading all the verses, he knew he hadn't been doing his part in giving.

Consider inviting family members to see the work of one of the ministries you want to support or one they might be interested in supporting. They may experience a change of heart when they see how great the needs are or the life-changing work of the ministry.

Another option is to engage family in one of many Bible studies on generosity. For women, Women Doing Well Initiative's *Extravagant God* Bible study is a good choice. For family members who are readers, several books may open their minds and hearts. Short and straightforward, *The Treasure Principle* is approachable even for those who don't like to read.

Family members may be interested in helping a ministry in a career or geographic area they have experience with. For example, if your husband works in IT, he may enthusiastically fund IT projects at a ministry (and almost all of them need this). If he once lived in Thailand, he may have an interest in supporting organizations that fight human trafficking. Has he considered how he has received help from people that he would like to pass on to others? Or how has he needed help but not received it?

Many times the example we set can be the greatest influence on our family. A friend of mine, Lacie, enjoys spontaneous giving; she seeks to be ready for the Holy Spirit's promptings. She also has experienced the joy of giving money to strangers, learning that God was using her to meet needs. Often her son Mark was with her, rolling his eyes. Then her example began to influence him.

One morning, Mark jumped in the car with Lacie and asked if they could stop at a local convenience store on the way to school. He explained that he wanted to give some cream soda to a young man who worked at the store. Lacie looked at him, puzzled. Mark said he had been in the store to buy a six-pack of cream soda and had struck up a conversation with the cashier, who had never heard of cream soda. Mark enjoyed the cashier's surprise when he delivered the gift, and he left the store with a smile. Now he enjoys collaborating with his mom on opportunities to give spontaneously.

Although you may not be able to give like you want from your family's financial resources without creating strife within the family, you can give a favorite piece of clothing, jewelry, books, or something else you now own. Such gifts can touch someone's heart. In addition, your possessions could be donated to a charity auction.

Paying the groceries of someone who's waiting in line demonstrates generosity (and embarrasses our teenagers). Secretly paying for the meal of a family at a restaurant is also an opportunity to give (and is less embarrassing to our teenagers).

Our family members are "under development," just as we are, with the Master Transformer at work, the Holy Spirit. We need to be patient, encouraging, and prayerful with our family members, as God is with us.

CHAPTER 16

Giving with Friends

Anne, Rosemary, Laurie, Judi, and I worked together in the law department of a corporation early in my career. We became good friends and took trips annually: a girls' weekend away. In the early years, we talked a lot about men, careers, and demanding work schedules. As we grew older, our conversation topics changed to menopause, aging parents, and loss of memory. In the next stage of life, our conversation will likely include Medicare, adult diapers, and the loss of our hearing. We laugh as we "do life" together.

We are made for community. As Christians, we worship, study, and pray together. We serve others together. We share many events, decisions, and challenges. So, why do we often make money decisions alone? Why is money a sensitive subject to discuss outside the family and even sometimes within the family? Money is just a tool, right?

From generation to generation, we pass on family attitudes about money. Did you grow up in a family that had little but tried to mask it? Or a family that had little, and it was a source of tension? The family you grew up in may have had surplus, but you learned to save for a rainy day, because one can never save too much. Or you may have been taught that it isn't polite to talk about money outside the family.

Our culture sends the message that money is important and personal. Discussing money exposes us to unpredictable reactions from others. Some of us fear envy or the expectations of others. Or we fear criticism of our use of money. We wonder if others think we're earning more or less than the value of our work. Do others expect us to shoulder more responsibility—for everything from the Girl Scout cookie sales to the church budget? And we may fear being "loved" or "included" just because we have money.

Money is one of the most challenging topics to discuss in our churches, but it's one of the most discussed subjects in the Bible. By not talking about living faithfully with money, we miss the great joy of being on the journey together. Paul recognized his need for being in community. He wrote to the church in Rome that when he came he wanted to encourage them in their faith, but he said he also needed to be encouraged (Romans 1:12).

Wait. Didn't Jesus instruct us not to do our good deeds publicly, saying, "Do not let your left hand know what your right hand is doing" (Matthew 6:3)? Yes, and later in the same passage, he instructed the disciples to pray behind closed doors. Yet we pray with others openly when we gather. Also Jesus tells us to "let your light shine before others, that they may see your good deeds and glorify your Father in heaven" (Matthew 5:16)?

The key is our *motivation*. In Matthew 5, Jesus encouraged the disciples to let the light lead to good deeds and ultimately to the praise of the Father. In Matthew 6, Jesus said we should be careful not to be like the hypocrites, who did their good deeds to be praised by others, rather than directing their praise to the Father. Is the good deed self-focused or God-focused? Does our discussion of giving lead to glorifying God or ourselves?

God created us to be in relationship with each other and with him. We're made for community, not life as lone rangers. Our good deeds encourage each other. We are rejuvenated when we learn from others who are farther along on this journey. We are encouraged by their transparency about their lives, including their successes and failures.

Ways to Give in Community

Community comes in many forms. For some, community is a small group focused on giving. Others are dedicated to discipleship more broadly. Others are devoted to a particular mission or need, and they offer time and money.

Jeff Rutt, a successful homebuilder in Pennsylvania, started the nonprofit called Homes for Hope in 2007 (homes4hope.org). Local contractors shared his vision of ending poverty and worked together, donating their time to build homes. When the homes are sold, profits are donated to organizations like HOPE International, a Christian microfinance organization serving the poor in other countries.

We also find companions at gatherings of Christians. Three events that provide safe places for encouragement and guidance are Generous Giving's Celebration of Generosity (generousgiving.org/annual -celebrations), Women Doing Well's Inspiring Generous Joy events (womendoingwell.org/events/events), and The Gathering (the gathering.com).

Another opportunity to engage in community is a Journey of Generosity retreat held locally (generousgiving.org/small-gatherings). Each retreat is a twenty-four-hour chance to join with peers in a retreat setting to discuss financial stewardship and explore the fullness of God's joy through living generous lives. Although the emphasis is on giving, no one asks for money or suggests where or how much to give. It's just a place to talk about some of the challenges with giving and to celebrate God's generous heart together.

Consider building community through creating a Giving Circle, a group that pools individual members' money to create a group fund. Together, you decide where to give the pooled amount. Participants often donate their time to the ministries they select as they increase their knowledge of the ministry and its needs. In 2008 more than five hundred Giving Circles were in operation.[1]

Strike Force 421, a Giving Circle in Fort Lauderdale, Florida, was created on April 21 (hence the *421*). One of the founders, Patti, heard about Giving Circles when she attended a Journey of Generosity at the invitation of a friend. She left excited about the possibility of forming one and met with three other women over lunch to plan the beginning of a circle.

The circle would eventually include one hundred women, each giving $1,000 each year to the pooled fund. Currently, members meet twice a year, once to hear ministries share their needs and the other to award the grant. Between the meetings, members conduct site visits and complete evaluations for all members to review.

When asked what the hardest part of forming Strike Force 421 was, Patti laughed and said that at the first lunch of the four organizers, three were lawyers. "Can you imagine what it was like to get three lawyers to agree on the rules?"

On one occasion, women were preparing the meal for a Strike Force 421 gathering, and Patti and Kathy went to a grocery store to buy food for it. Patti challenged Kathy to pay the grocery bill of the woman in line behind them. Kathy rose to the challenge, and to her surprise, the woman said that she knew she was to allow Kathy to give to her, because of a devotional she'd read that morning. What was the devotional? *God Calling*, coedited and rewritten by Patti and a friend.[2]

Mission trips can often generate interest in giving. Many churches sponsor such trips, and many ministries sponsor and encourage trips to come see their work. The relationships made or deepened on a trip can be the basis for a group that shares a passion for the ministry and wants to continue to support it. Instead of returning to your routines after such a trip, take the next step with the group to consider how you can continue supporting that ministry.

Finding community doesn't require starting a new group. A small group, Bible study gathering, a group of close friends, or any other group can be a community that helps us and our friends grow in stewarding God's blessings.

Being in community is not optional. We can't deal with our fears and uncertainties alone. Scott Bader-Saye writes, "Courage requires community, both for the learning of it and for the living of it."[3] We need to be in community to remain courageous. And when we give in community, we discover joys and surprises along the way. And who doesn't want more joy?

CHAPTER 17

Giving with a Twist

Giving can be done with a little creativity, which can make it both more satisfying and more effective. There are ways to get others involved in giving, to ensure that funds are used wisely, and to have fun by giving spontaneously.

Catherine received an email from one of her favorite ministries about a need for a new truck in Uganda. They also needed sewing machines for classes in which they taught girls and young women how to sew as a potential source of income. Catherine believed God was leading her to give toward those needs, but not the full $50,000 needed. So she decided to offer a matching gift: she would give a dollar for every dollar others gave toward this need, to a maximum of $25,000. She hoped her offer would prompt others to give generously.

The ministry sent an email to those on its donor list, sharing the matching gift offer. Shortly afterward, Catherine received an email from the ministry that they had received half of the $25,000 in a matter of minutes from *one* donor. When she asked, "Really?" the caller replied, "Your good friend Elizabeth called to pledge the amount. She thought it was a great idea. Plus, she said jokingly she wanted to make sure you had to pony up that money."

Amused, Catherine said, "That's just like Elizabeth. I'm grateful for her support."

Offering a Match

What is a match? A donor offers to match each dollar given by donors during a certain period, up to a certain maximum amount. Donors like matches, because every dollar they give is doubled. Ministries like matches, because they encourage people to give.

A match can be used to encourage current donors to give more, or new donors to join in the giving. If you offer a match, be sure to specify the conditions.

When proposing a match, you will probably work with the recipient organization to consider the time frame in which donors must give to earn the match, whether both cash and noncash donations are counted against the match, the sources of donations (previous donors or new donors only), and whether donations designated for a particular purpose count toward the match.

Funding Expert Advice

Many ministries need specific expert advice, such as on legal or tax matters, fundraising, technology, risk management, investments, security, strategic planning, or leadership and employee development. Paying for expert advice can fall to the bottom of the list for a nonprofit, even when it would be wise in the long run to invest in the expert advice right away. You could consider donating a gift to help a nonprofit hire an expert. Expert advice may improve the ministry's efficiency or effectiveness exponentially.

Child Sponsorship

A popular method of fundraising is soliciting a donor to "sponsor" a child. Typically a donor commits to making monthly financial contributions. When considering sponsorship programs, find out how much of your donation is going directly to the child and the child's family, how much is being used for community development activities of the ministry, and how much is going to the costs of administration. You may also want to know if the local church is working with the ministry in its activities, and if not, why not.

Often child-sponsorship organizations allow donors to write to the children they sponsor. At one point I was writing to twelve children all over the world. I felt like the old woman who lived in a shoe.

In Honor of a Loved One

Sarah and her sister were regular contributors to the work of Every Village in South Sudan, particularly to funding its radio ministry. Each year, Every Village had a campaign to raise money to buy solar-powered radios for the South Sudanese, who would hear broadcasts from Every Village radio towers manned by local Sudanese.

When Sarah's sister died unexpectedly in an automobile accident, she wanted to honor her in a special way with a large donation, knowing she would have to trust God to provide for her future financial needs if she did. She decided to honor her sister, who had a heart for the South Sudanese, by funding a new radio tower that would broadcast the radio programs to additional villages. She knows she can expect to see the smile on her sister's face someday.

A Gift Occasion

A friend who shared my compassion for children decided to give me a unique birthday gift: she sponsored a little girl who had the same birthday as mine. On my birthday, she gave me a birthday card with the little girl's photo and information. I loved it!

Meet Individual Needs

Often our paths cross the paths of those who have needs.

Nolan and Danny run a local yoga studio, so they understood the benefits of yoga and meditation for those who were stressed. They wanted to offer yoga and meditation in schools for teachers and troubled children, so they did the preliminary work and tested the impact. But how were they to make a living if they spent part of their time on this project? A friend stepped in to help support them for a year, as did others.

Denise's husband divorced her, and in the property settlement he took her only vehicle. Without that vehicle, Denise couldn't support herself through her sales job. Leigh learned of the need and bought her a new car.

Janet is caring for ten foster children in her home alone. With that many children, Janet can't work a full-time job. Kathy makes financial contributions to Janet to help her raise those children.

Elizabeth's daughter was leaving for college, but her daughter's best friend wasn't, because her family didn't have the financial resources for college. Elizabeth and her husband stepped in to pay for her college tuition.

In 2016, Louisiana suffered from catastrophic flooding, even in areas that had never flooded before. Lindsey heard about it at a reunion of camp friends. Heather, one of those friends, posted a request to her friends on Facebook, asking that each send even the smallest amount to help a local friend who lost both her home and her business. When Lindsey read the request, she didn't think twice about writing a check to send to Heather. Lindsey initially thought of sending a few hundred dollars, but then felt prompted to send $10,000. She asked Heather to distribute her gift to those in need however she thought best. Lindsey learned later that the amount needed to repair the home and business of the hairdresser was $10,000.

Donate Possessions

I used to purchase inexpensive but nice artwork from local artists when I traveled. When my walls became full, I switched to coffee cups. I now have both with no place in my home and no real use. What do we do with things we can't use?

Many nonprofits have annual auctions, and you may be surprised at the items they're interested in auctioning. Although you don't want to give them your junk, be cautious in reaching a conclusion on the definition of *junk*. One person's trash is another person's treasure. Simply ask ministries if they have an auction and what items they're interested in. You can donate items, such as collections that you've lost interest in or space for. How many sets of dishes, towels, and sheets do you need to keep?

Animal shelters need animal supplies. Ministries to children often need toys and other supplies. Most nonprofits benefit from office supplies. Consider developing the practice of donating one thing every time you purchase another.

Share Your Home

Jane and Steve built a home with five bedrooms for their family of five. Even before their three daughters grew up and moved out, they were offering the guest bedroom and other unused space to those who needed a place to stay. Their guests were often runaway teenagers, young adults starting out on their own, university students, those who had lost their jobs, and the ill who needed care. Jane said, "Steve would come home every night after work and ask, 'Who's sleeping here tonight?'"

Support Someone Else's God-Given Dream

Emily loves to study Scripture and longs for other women to be touched by excellent Bible teaching. She recognized that some women aren't able to attend Bible study on a Sunday morning and that many don't feel comfortable in a church building. Emily used her savings to start a unique Bible study event: a lunchtime Bible study at the local country club, led by an outstanding Bible teacher. Women who work are able to come during their lunch break. Some invite unchurched friends and colleagues to join them in a comfortable environment. Emily provided the financial support to cover the costs.

These are just a few of the many ways we can give. As we grow in experience, we will have our own creative ideas. As we meet others who take their giving seriously, we learn of other ways to give. This is part of the adventure.

PART 5

The Adventure
of Giving

CHAPTER 18

The (Unexpected?)
Blessings of Giving

As we surrender all to our generous God, we are swept into God's activity in the world. For some, the adventure includes foreign places and cultures. For example, Peter and Shauna lived in mud huts in South Sudan because of their love for the South Sudanese. Among other hardships, they slept under nets to protect themselves from scorpions.

Jim is a young social worker who travels to Uganda to work with former child soldiers and victims of the Lord's Resistance Army. He has had to run from rebel armies along with those he serves.

Addie weekly visits and helps those with AIDS. Terry works with prisoners to prepare them for work after their release. Chris tutors a child after school. Maria teaches English to new immigrants. Susan provides pro bono legal services to abused women. Caroline, a doctor, participates in annual mission trips to provide medical care in places of need.

For others, the adventure is starting or running a business, helping local children to learn to read, teaching job skills to former prisoners, mentoring young adults, serving on the board of directors for a Christian nonprofit, or showing compassion to those dying of cancer.

These individuals aren't the only ones called to live an adventurous life as part of God's story. Opportunities exist right where God has placed each of us in our own communities. In addition, we can support those who go, whether it is to the other side of town or to the other side of the world. We who pray and give, and encourage others to pray and give, are *partners* with these men and women and with God. We too are swept into God's movement. We aren't to sit on the sidelines or view our contributions as insignificant. We are to join them in God's mission—and along the way there are many blessings.

Freedom

We experience freedom as we focus on a purpose or mission that's greater than ourselves. Giving leads us to lift our gaze from ourselves—and beyond our families—to view the faces of others who are in need and are beautiful in God's sight too. We experience freedom from the self-centeredness our culture promotes.

And as we give, we let go of what holds us. We are freed from depending on ourselves for our security. We let go of our drive to control. We let go of interpreting blessings as God's approval, and we let go of the fear of losing those blessings. So we learn to let go and live in freedom.

Joy

We were made in God's image, and as his daughters, we're hardwired to experience joy in giving as God does. When Jesus had dinner at Zacchaeus's house, Zacchaeus announces an amazing decision (Luke 19:1-10). He was going to return what he improperly collected *and* give away half of what he owned to the poor. (I wonder what Mrs. Zacchaeus was thinking.)

Was Zacchaeus attempting to impress his friends? I think not. His friends probably thought he was crazy. We don't know what Jesus said at dinner, but he demonstrated God's love for Zacchaeus and gave him a much-needed sense of who he was made to be. We can almost feel Zacchaeus's joy. And we too will experience great joy as we grow in our relationship with God through generosity.

Increasing Faith

God is not short of money, so why does he want *us* to do the giving? Because when we live generously, we grow in our relationship with him, and we learn we can trust him.

I hadn't realized how low my expectations of God were until I heard the story of a house in Haiti. In the fall of 2012, Rich and Janet made a trip to Haiti to help Haitians after torrential storms caused flooding. Those at my church praying for them received photos of the flood damage. One specific photo struck my heart, a photo of a house, the poorest and smallest of structures, leaning at a sixty- to seventy-degree angle and about to collapse. In this house lived three generations of a family, including one mentally disabled child. I asked, "How could those who have nothing lose what they have?"

I sent a gift, but I couldn't imagine how my gift could help that family. Weeks later, I saw Rich and Janet at church. They were waiting for me after the worship service with big smiles. Janet said, "We couldn't wait to tell you about the fishes and the loaves!" Rich then explained that the gift inspired local residents to offer help by providing labor and materials, resulting in the repair not only of that one house, but also of three others nearby.

In the book of Ephesians, we are told that God "is able to do immeasurably more than all we ask or imagine, according to his power that is at work within us" (Ephesians 3:20). He certainly did in this case.

A Legacy

Lydia is the first recorded follower of Jesus in Europe (Acts 16:11-15, 40). Paul had received a vision of a man calling him to come to Macedonia. He and Luke caught a ship to Philippi, a Roman colony and the leading city in that region. While looking for a place of prayer, they met Lydia outside the city by a river. Lydia, a worshiper of God, was a successful businesswoman dealing in purple cloth. She insisted that Paul and his friends stay with her and generously provided for their needs. As a result of their meeting, all those in her household were baptized. She also used her affluence and influence to help Paul on his first journey to Europe.

So how did God use her willingness to give? He blessed her family, but he also multiplied her gift in a way she could not have seen. The Pew Research Center estimated that in 2010 the number of Christians in Europe was over 565 million.[1] It all started with Paul letting the Spirit lead him to Europe, followed by one woman's response—all part of God's plan for Paul, for Lydia, and for Europe.

Like Lydia, we may not have the opportunity to see the full impact of our generosity, and it may go largely unrecognized in our lifetime. Our hope is to see the faces of individuals we've never met but were helped in part through our willingness to give. Can you imagine that moment of joy and celebration?

The desire for lasting impact is present from generation to generation. The world is full of monuments stemming from humankind's desire for legacy. They pay tribute to titanic conquests, victories, accomplishments, and discoveries. Today we name buildings on college campuses and in city centers in honor of those who want to be remembered. Prizes and scholarship funds often memorialize individuals or families.

A Christian's legacy, however, is the impact for the kingdom of God. Jesus taught his disciples, "You did not choose me, but I chose you and appointed you so that you might go and bear fruit—fruit that will last" (John 15:16). A kingdom legacy impacts *people*; it's not about stamping buildings with our names. And it's likely we won't fully know our legacy until our days on earth are over and Jesus shares it with us.

Freedom, joy, faith, and significance—this is the abundant life we were promised (John 10:10). And who doesn't want that?

CHAPTER 19

The Rest of the Story

Lunch had just arrived when my cell phone rang. I was at a seminar relevant to my practice of law and was at a nearby restaurant. I glanced at the unfamiliar number and decided to answer. "Kim, hello! This is David Gallagher calling from Kenya," the caller said with elation. "I'm just calling to thank you for your incredibly generous gift to Open Arms International!" He continued, "I can't tell you how much this gift means to us and how it is such an answer to prayer. So I just wanted to personally call to thank you." I'm not sure what David said next, because at that point my fifty-four-year-old memory had begun running through the files in my brain, trying to reconcile his enthusiasm with the small donation I'd made to Open Arms.

I had been introduced to Open Arms at a morning breakfast hosted by the Barnabas Group. While sipping my coffee, I had listened to David describe their ministry to rescue and raise abandoned children in Eldoret, Kenya. I felt compassion for those children, so I decided to give a modest gift while committing to learn more about the ministry. My contribution to Open Arms was made through my Giving Fund at National Christian Foundation. As I sat waiting for the waiter to bring my check for lunch, I thought, *Wow, the US dollar must go a long way in Kenya.*

But the more I reflected on David's call, the more I grew uneasy. Something was not adding up.

I sent a quick email to the National Christian Foundation of Houston to ask my contact whether she could confirm the amount I'd sent to Open Arms. She said she would check, but added she remembered it was a large amount. As I made my way back to the conference room, I heard the familiar beep telling me a new email had arrived. I stopped abruptly when I read that the amount was *one hundred* times what I'd intended. Gulp. I thanked her and hung up. "Lord, I just gave away a whole lot of your money."

I continued to receive emails from those associated with Open Arms, thanking me for my gift and praising me for my generosity and faithfulness. I repeatedly tried to explain: "No, you don't understand. God did this. I had nothing to do with it." Believe me. I had *nothing* to do with it. Really.

Finally, I concluded I needed to share my mistake with David, so they wouldn't think so highly of me. After hearing my story, he responded as I expected, insisting on the return of the amount above my intended gift. Amazingly, his graciousness exceeded his previous enthusiasm. I asked for time to pray for direction.

For the remainder of the day, I was present at the conference in body only.

In praying about the gift to Open Arms that evening, I remembered the commitment I'd made at my first Celebration of Generosity four years earlier. I had pledged to God that I would give half of my salary for that year during the *next* year.

At that moment, God winked. The contribution was the same amount as my commitment. So I didn't experience God's disappointment or displeasure for not having fulfilled that earlier promise.

Instead, I received God's gentle assurance that he knows me—and he walks with me on this journey of giving.

So, what have I learned?

By not stepping into how Jesus is leading us to follow him, we shortchange ourselves. We will never fully be who we were designed to be until we follow Christ wherever he leads us. We will never experience security or happiness deeply until we cease striving to meet these needs in any place other than following Jesus. Otherwise, we live small lives, trying to control our surroundings and seeking to fill our needs ourselves. We weren't made for this way of living; we were made for adventure.

Giving opens the way for us to see God at work in the world—and to be with him in this adventure. Living a life of generosity unlocks the pathway to joy. The more we give, the greater the adventure—and the greater the adventure, the greater the joy.

Acknowledgments

I wish to thank my family and friends who patiently encouraged and supported me as I wrote this book.

Thanks to those with Women Doing Well, who invited me on the journey with them after their pilot event in Houston. I'm grateful, too, to Lloyd Bentsen III and John Montgomery for inviting me to my first Celebration of Generosity.

A special thank you to Cindy Bunch at InterVarsity Press, who was willing to take a chance on a newbie like me, as well as to Anna Haggard and Ethan McCarthy, for the many ways they helped make the manuscript better.

APPENDIX A

Further Reading

Generosity

Revolution in Generosity: Transforming Stewards to Be Rich Toward God, edited by Wesley K. Willmer

Women and Philanthropy: Boldly Shaping a Better World by Sondra Shaw-Hardy and Martha A. Taylor, with Buffy Beaudoin-Schwartz

Passing the Plate: Why American Christians Don't Give Away More Money by Christian Smith and Michael O. Emerson, with Patricia Snell

The Generous Soul: An Introduction to Missional Giving by Marty Duren

The Treasure Principle: Unlocking the Secret of Joyful Giving by Randy Alcorn

The Generosity Bet: Secrets of Risk, Reward, and Real Joy by William F. High with Ashley B. McCauley

The Generosity Factor: Discover the Joy of Giving Your Time, Talent, and Treasure by Ken Blanchard and S. Truett Cathy

Abundant: Experiencing the Incredible Journey of Generosity by Todd Harper

The Genius of Generosity: Lessons from a Secret Pact Between Two Friends by Chip Ingram

The Paradox of Generosity: Giving We Receive, Grasping We Lose by Christian Smith and Hilary Davidson

How Much Is Enough? Hungering for God in an Affluent Culture by Arthur Simon

God and Money: How We Discovered True Riches at Harvard Business School by John Cortines and Gregory Baumer

I Like Giving: The Transforming Power of a Generous Life by Brad Formsma

How to Be Rich: It's Not What You Have. It's What You Do with What You Have by Andy Stydy Stanley

NIV Stewardship, Study Bible: Discover God's Design for Life, the Environment, Finances, and Generosity Eternity (Zondervan)

Purpose and Passion

Living a Purpose-Full Life: What Happens When You Say Yes to God by Jan Johnson

Second Calling: Finding Passion and Purpose for the Rest of Your Life by Dale Hanson Bourke

The On-Purpose Person: Making Your Life Make Sense by Kevin W. McCarthy

Wholehearted Purpose by Mary Tomlinson

Listen: Finding God in the Story of Your Life by Keri Wyatt Kent

Find Your Passion: 25 Questions You Must Ask Yourself by Henri Junttila

Giving Wisely

Don't Just Give It Away: How to Make the Most of Your Charitable Giving by Renata J. Rafferty

Connected for Good: A Gameplan for a Generous Life by John Stanley

Practical Generosity: How to Choose Between Spending, Saving, and Giving by Shane Enete

The Generosity Plan: Sharing Your Time, Treasure, and Talent to Shape the World by Kathy LeMay

Master Your Money: A Step-by-Step Plan for Experiencing Financial Contentment by Ron Blue with Michael Blue

The Art of Giving: Where the Soul Meets a Business Plan by Charles Bronfman and Jeffrey Solomon

The Age of Global Giving: A Practical Guide for Donors and Funding Recipients of Our Time by Gilles Gravelle

Giving Wisely: Killing with Kindness or Empowering Lasting Transformation? by Jonathan Martin

The Eternity Portfolio, Illuminated: A Practical Guide to Investing Your Money for Ultimate Results by Alan Gotthardt

Giving 2.0: Transform Your Giving and Our World by Laura Arrillaga-Andreessen

Give Smart: Philanthropy That Gets Results by Thomas J. Tierney and Joel L. Fleishman

"Questions to Ask Charities Before Donating: Tips for How to Investigate a Charity's Results" on charitynavigator.org

Expenses and Gifts Snapshot Tabulation

Appearance

_____ New clothes and shoes, cleaning

_____ Hair, skin, and nails care, and products

_____ Other

Auto (repeat for each automobile)

_____ Auto insurance

_____ Auto maintenance/ repair

_____ Gasoline

_____ Parking/tolls

_____ Other

Work Expenses (not reimbursed)

_____ Dues/fees

_____ Continuing education

_____ Memberships

_____ Supplies

_____ Other

Education

_____ Tuition

_____ Books and supplies

_____ Room and board

_____ Other

Entertainment

_____ Eating out	_____ Games
_____ Dinner parties	_____ Books/magazines
_____ Internet apps and services	_____ Sports/arts
_____ Music/movies	_____ Other

Food

_____ Delivery	_____ Groceries

Giving

_____ Gifts to family members

_____ Gifts to others

_____ Giving—tax-deductible (but not through a DAF)

_____ Giving—not tax-deductible

_____ Assistance to parents (paid directly to vendor)

_____ Assistance to parents (not paid directly to vendor)

_____ Expenses incurred in connection with charitable work

_____ Other

Health

_____ Health insurance premiums	_____ Therapy/counseling
	_____ Trainer/health club
_____ Doctor bills/tests	_____ Long-term care policy premiums
_____ Prescriptions/vaccinations	_____ Other

House (repeat for each home)

_____ Modifications/repairs/maintenance

_____ Furnishings

_____ Property taxes

_____ Casualty insurance/flood insurance premiums
_____ Utilities (natural gas, electricity, water)
_____ Home security
_____ Cable television
_____ Telephone/cell phone service/Internet
_____ Lawn care/pool care/housekeeping
_____ Other

Pets

_____ Sitting/boarding   _____ Supplies/training
_____ Vet/meds   _____ Other

Professional Advisers

_____ Attorney   _____ Financial
_____ Tax   _____ Other

Travel

_____ Recreational   _____ Work travel (if not
_____ Visiting family   reimbursed)
_____ Visiting friends   _____ Other

Miscellaneous

_____ Mail/delivery services   _____ Care of parents
_____ Umbrella liability policy _____ Memberships not
premiums   included above

Charitable and Ministry Activities

Creation Care

_____ Animals	_____ Zoos and parks
_____ Environment protection	_____ Conservation

Evangelism

_____ Missionaries	_____ Media
_____ Church planting	_____ Training and education
_____ Bible translation/	_____ Campus ministries
distribution	_____ Workplace ministries

Government and Culture

_____ Public education	_____ Institutions of higher
_____ Media	learning
_____ Museums/music/	_____ Political parties and
performing arts	candidates
_____ Visual arts	

_____ Legislation/regulations/
judicial reform

Justice/Freedom/Peacemaking

_____ Human trafficking and slavery

_____ Peacemaking

_____ Rights/equal opportunity

_____ Pornography/sexual exploitation

_____ Unplanned pregnancy

_____ Immigration and immigrants

_____ Religious freedom

_____ Veterans

_____ Orphans/abused children

_____ Elderly

Medical/Health

_____ Medical research

_____ Emergency medical relief

_____ Prevention of diseases and illnesses

_____ Medical missionaries

_____ Medical supplies and equipment

_____ Medical and health training/education

_____ Physical and mental illness/disabilities

_____ Clean water

_____ Substance abuse

_____ End of life care

Poverty Alleviation

_____ Improving agriculture

_____ Development of local businesses

_____ Micro savings and loans

_____ Emergency provision of basic needs

_____ Housing

_____ Education and training

_____ Fair trade and wages

_____ Homeless

_____ Debt relief

_____ Rehabilitation of
formerly incarcerated

_____ Single parent support

The Church

_____ Healthy families

_____ Healthy marriages

_____ Ministry to singles

_____ Youth

_____ Children

_____ Young adults/college
students

_____ Seniors

_____ Stewardship

_____ Christian camps/
retreats

_____ Church mission trips
and local mission
activities

_____ Spiritual formation and
direction

_____ Underfunded small
churches

_____ Pastoral care and
training

_____ Christian education/
seminaries

_____ Other

Values or Standards

Below is a list of values that we may all share, but that we would each prioritize differently. The values we prioritize most highly are likely to be the ones we expect an organization to value as well.

Looking at the list below, ask yourself how you would complete the following. *I value _____, _____, and _____ as my highest priorities and would expect an organization I give to to value them as well.* One way to determine your top priorities is to eliminate those of lesser importance until only three are left.

Transparency	Integrity	Innovation	Ethics
Inclusiveness	Communication	Prayerfulness	Excellence
Learning	Improvement	Humility	Efficiency
Effectiveness	Organization	Clarity	Hard work
Collaboration	Loyalty	Faithfulness	Endurance
Perseverance	Compassion	Mercy	Commitment
Forgiveness	Patience	Respect	Frugality
Wisdom	Experience	Compliance	Planning
Knowledge	Experimentation	Impact	Passion
Initiative	Relationships	Thoughtfulness	Reflection

Initiative	Intelligence	Honesty	Creativity
Productivity	Truth	Optimism	Open-mindedness
Goodness	Sincerity	Patience	
Kindness	Service	Kindness	
Realism	Strategy	Selflessness	

Example of an Annual Giving Plan

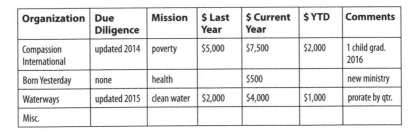

Organization	Due Diligence	Mission	$ Last Year	$ Current Year	$ YTD	Comments
Compassion International	updated 2014	poverty	$5,000	$7,500	$2,000	1 child grad. 2016
Born Yesterday	none	health		$500		new ministry
Waterways	updated 2015	clean water	$2,000	$4,000	$1,000	prorate by qtr.
Misc.						

Column 1: What's the name of the organization or ministry that will receive funds, either directly from you or your Giving Fund?

Column 2: When has due diligence been done on this ministry? Was it adequate? Does it need updating?

Column 3: What is the mission of the ministry? Is it consistent with how you believe God would have you to give? Does it bear a relationship to your purpose and passion?

Column 4: What did you give last year to this ministry?

Column 5: What do you plan to give this year?

Column 6: What have you given this year to date?

Column 7: Include any helpful comments here.

Notes

Foreword

[1]Debra J. Mesch, *Women Give 2010: New Research About Women and Giving* (Indianapolis: Center on Philanthropy at Indiana University, 2010), scholar works.iupui.edu/bitstream/handle/1805/6337/women_give_2010_report.pdf.
[2]Debra Mesch, "The Gender Gap in Charitable Giving," *Wall Street Journal,* February 1, 2016, www.wsj.com/articles/the-gender-gap-in-charitable -giving-1454295689.
[3]Michelle Lodge, "Dispelling Myths About Women and Charitable Giving," *Fortune,* October 20, 2014, www.fortune.com/2014/10/20/dispelling-myths -about-women-and-charitable-giving.
[4]Ibid.

1 The Impact of One Woman

[1]See David Grant Gallagher, *Our Daddy Who Art in Heaven: God Is Closer than You Think* (self-published, 2016).
[2]"The Texas Response to Human Trafficking," Office of the Attorney General, Texas, 10, www.texasattorneygeneral.gov/files/agency/human _trafficking_2008.pdf.

2 What God Has Placed in Women's Hands

[1]Claudia Goldin, "The Role of World War II in the Rise of Women's Work" (NBER Working Paper Series, no. 3203, National Bureau of Economic Research, Cambridge, MA, 1989), www.nber.org/papers/w3203.pdf.

[2]*Women Give 2012: New Research about Women and Giving* (Indianapolis: Women's Philanthropy Institute, August 2012), 4, www.ncdsv.org/images /WPI_WomenGive2012NewResearchAboutWomenAndGivign_8-2012. pdf.

[3]*Financial Concerns of Women*, BMO Wealth Institute, 2015, 2, www.bmo .com/privatebank/pdf/Q1-2015-Wealth-Institute-Report-Financial -Concerns-of-Women.pdf.

[4]"More Working Women Than Men Have College Degrees, Census Bureau Reports," *United States Census Bureau*, April 2011, www.census.gov /newsroom/releases/archives/education/cb11-72.html.

[5]Amy L. Sherman, *Directions in Women's Giving 2012* (Richardson, TX: Women Doing Well, 2012), 14. See womendoingwell.org to purchase a full report and review the executive summary.

[6]Cathy Benko and Bill Pelster, "How Women Decide," *Harvard Business Review*, September 2013, hbr.org/2013/09/how-women-decide.

[7]*Goal III Report: An Annual Report on Women's Advancement into Leadership Positions within the American Bar Association* (Chicago: American Bar Association—Commission on Women in the Profession, 2016), 4, www .americanbar.org/content/dam/aba/administrative/women/2016_goal3 _women.authcheckdam.pdf.

[8]"Distribution of Physicians by Gender," The Henry J. Kaiser Family Foun- dation, last modified April 2016, www.kff.org/other/state-indicator /physicians-by-gender/.

[9]Jenny Hope, "Women Doctors Will Soon Outnumber Men After Numbers in Medical School Go Up Ten-fold," *Daily Mail*, November 30, 2011, www.dailymail.co.uk/health/article-2067887/Women-doctors-soon-outnumber -men-numbers-medical-school-fold.html.

[10]"Women and Business—The Present Equation," Women Entrepreneurs UK, 2010, www.womenentrepreneursuk.com/women-in-business.htm.

[11]"Launching Women-Owned Businesses on to a High Growth Trajectory," National Women's Business Council, 1, accessed May 10, 2016, www.nwbc .gov/research/launching-women-owned-businesses-high-growth-trajectory.

[12] *The 2015 State of Women-Owned Businesses Report, American Express OPEN*, 2015, 1, www.womenable.com/content/userfiles/Amex_OPEN _State_of_WOBs_2015_Executive_Report_finalsm.pdf.

[13] "More Female Millionaires in Portugal," *Algarve Daily News*, November 26, 2013, www.algarvedailynews.com/news/666-more-femail-mil lionaries-in-portugal.

[14] Wendy Wang and Kim Parker, "Record Share of Americans Have Never Married as Values, Economics and Gender Patterns Change," *Pew Research Center*, September 24, 2014, www.pewsocialtrends.org/2014/09/24/record -share-of-americans-have-never-married/.

[15] Casey E. Copen, et al., "First Marriages in the United States: Data From the 2006–2010 National Survey of Family Growth," *National Health Statistics Reports*, no. 49, March 2012, 5, www.cdc.gov/nchs/data/nhsr /nhsr049.pdf.

[16] Jiaquan Xu, et al., "Deaths: Final Data for 2013," *National Vital Statistics Reports* 64:2 (February 2016), 6, www.cdc.gov/nchs/data/nvsr/nvsr64 /nvsr64_02.pdf.

[17] Prudential, "Financial Experience & Behaviors Among Women: 2014-2015 Prudential Research Study" (Newark, NJ: Prudential Insurance Company of America, 2014), 6, www.prudential.com/media/managed/wm/media/Pru _Women_Study_2014.pdf.

[18] Sondra Shaw-Hardy and Martha A. Taylor, with Buffy Beaudoin-Schwartz, *Women and Philanthropy: Boldly Shaping a Better World* (San Francisco: Jossey-Bass, 2010), 12-14.

[19] Ibid., 23, 109.

[20] Sherman, *Directions in Women's Giving*, 12-13.

[21] Ibid., 12.

[22] Shaw-Hardy and Taylor, *Women and Philanthropy*, 7, 17.

[23] Ibid., 15.

[24] "Our Founders," Women Moving Millions, accessed May 1, 2016, www .womenmovingmillions.org/who-we-are/our-founders/.

[25] Women Moving Millions, *All In for Her: A Call to Action*, www.allinforher .org/sites/default/files/ALL_IN_FOR_HER-A_Call_To_Action.pdf.

[26] Ibid., 4. 1.7 percent is the lowest percentage in the forty years prior to 2013.

[27] Jacki Zehner, "Transformative Wealth from Women, for Women," *Stanford Social Innovation Review*, October 9, 2014, www.ssir.org/articles /entry/transformative_wealth_from_women_for_women.

[28] Michelle Lodge, "Dispelling Myths About Women and Charitable Giving," *Fortune*, October 20, 2014, www.fortune.com/2014/10/20/dispelling-myths -about-women-and-charitable-giving; *All In for Her*, 4.

[29] Sharla Langston (founder of Women Doing Well, LLC), interview by Kim King, telephone, July 13, 2015.

[30] Marian V. Liautaud, "Women Doing Well," *Today's Christian Woman*, March 2014, www.todayschristianwoman.com/articles/2014/march/women -doing-well.html.

[31] Sherman, *Directions in Women's Giving*, 6.

[32] Liautaud, "Women Doing Well."

[33] Sherman, *Directions in Women's Giving*, 35.

3 God's Invitation to Give

[1] Ron Blue with Jeremy White, *Splitting Heirs: Giving Your Money and Things to Your Children Without Ruining Their Lives* (Chicago: Northfield Publishing, 2004), 34; *QuickFacts* (US Census Bureau), https://census.gov /quickfacts.

[2] Blue and White, *Splitting Heirs*, 34. The authors ask a very probing question: Why did God give Americans so much wealth?

[3] Elizabeth Svoboda, "Hard-Wired for Giving," *The Wall Street Journal*, August 31, 2013, www.wsj.com/amp/articles/hardwired-for-giving -1377902081.

[4] "When is Enough … Enough? Why The Wealthy Can't Get Off the Treadmill," *UBS Investor Watch*, 6. www.ubs.com/content/dam/Wealth ManagementAmericas/documents/investor-watch-2Q2015.pdf.

4 Listening to God About Money

[1] "Directory of Charities and Nonprofit Organizations," GuideStar, accessed January 12, 2015, www.guidestar.org/nonprofit-directory/religion.aspx.

[2] Kevin Drum, *Anne-Marie Slaughter's Time-Saving Microwave Tips* (June 23, 2012), www.motherjones.com/kevindrum/2012/06/anne-marie -slaughters-time-saving-microwave-tips.

[3]Larry Kim, "Multitasking Is Killing Your Brain," Inc., July 15, 2015, www
.inc.com/larry-kim/why-multi-tasking-is-killing-your-brain.html.
[4]Roy F. Baumeister and John Tierney, *Willpower: Rediscovering the Greatest
Human Strength* (New York: Penguin, 2012), Kindle edition, chap. 4,
"Decision Fatigue."
[5]Peter Swann, interview with Kim King, Houston, July 29, 2015.

5 How Much Do I Give?

[1]Alan Gotthardt, *The Eternity Portfolio, Illuminated: A Practical Guide to
Investing Your Money for Ultimate Results* (Sisters, OR: Deep River Books,
2015), 73.
[2]"Women & Money: How to Take Charge," Fidelity, March 23, 2016, www
.fidelity.com/viewpoints/personal-finance/women-manage-money.
[3]Mahzarin R. Banaji and Anthony G. Greenwald, *Blindspot: Hidden Biases
of Good People* (New York: Delacorte Press, 2013), 119-22.
[4]C. S. Lewis, *Mere Christianity* (New York: Simon & Schuster, 1996), 82.

6 What Are My Values in Choosing Organizations to Give To?

[1]Steve Corbett and Brian Fikkert, *When Helping Hurts: How to Alleviate
Poverty Without Hurting the Poor . . . and Yourself* (Chicago: Moody Publishers, 2009).
[2]Ibid., 64.
[3]Ibid., 53.
[4]Ibid., 65.
[5]Ibid., 68.
[6]Ibid., 145.
[7]Ibid.
[8]Kaitlin Mulhere, "Deep-Pocket Donors," *Inside Higher Ed*, January 28,
2015, www.insidehighered.com/news/2015/01/28/2014-record-year-higher
-ed-donations.

7 What Is My God-Given Purpose and Passion?

[1]Ann Montgomery, interview by author, August 12, 2015. One of Ann's
heroes is Desmond Tutu. She was thrilled when she was able to be present
for the filming of a conversation between Tutu and the Dalai Lama. She

explains, "It was the one time that it paid off to be an introvert. The producers of the film insisted that everyone present be quiet."

[2]Peter Greer and Phil Smith, *The Poor Will Be Glad: Joining the Revolution to Lift the World Out of Poverty* (Grand Rapids: Zondervan, 2009).

[3]Richard Stearns, *The Hole in Our Gospel* (Nashville: Thomas Nelson, 2010), 114.

[4]"Drew Houston's Commencement Address," MIT News, June 7, 2013, news.mit.edu/2013/commencement-address-houston-0607.

9 How Do I Identify a Good Organization?

[1]Alan Gotthardt, *The Eternity Portfolio, Illuminated: A Practical Guide to Investing Your Money for Ultimate Results* (Sisters, OR: Deep River Books, 2015), 164.

[2]Peter Greer and Chris Horst with Anna Haggard, *Mission Drift: The Unspoken Crisis Facing Leaders, Charities, and Churches* (Bloomington, MN: Bethany House Publishers, 2014), 18.

[3]Jeffrey Gettleman, "Meant to Keep Malaria Out, Mosquito Nets Are Used to Haul Fish In," *New York Times*, January 24, 2015, www.nytimes .com/2015/01/25/world/africa/mosquito-nets-for-malaria-spawn-new -epidemic-overfishing.html.

[4]Indiana School of Philanthropy, Stanford University, and GiveWell.org are three sources of such information.

[5]Bruce Wydick, "Want to Change the World? Sponsor a Child," *Christianity Today*, June 14, 2013, www.christianitytoday.com/ct/2013/june/want -to-change-world-sponsor-child.html.

10 Challenge to Generosity 1: Fear

[1]"Status and Progress of Emergency Planning for Racially and Ethnically Diverse Communities in Greater Houston: Findings from Co-Educational Forums with Community and Response Organizations," Texas Health Institute, September 2012, 6, www.texashealthinstitute.org/uploads /1/3/5/3/13535548/thi_houston_case_on_diversity__preparedness_2012 _updated.pdf.

[2]Scott Bader-Saye, *Following Jesus in a Culture of Fear (The Christian Practice of Everyday Life)* (Grand Rapids: Brazos Press, 2007), 31.

[3]Ibid.

[4]James Sterngold, "Madoff Victims Recount the Long Road Back," *Wall Street Journal*, updated December 9, 2013, www.wsj.com/articles/SB10001 42405270230356020457924822165787860.

[5]John Carney, "America Lost $10.2 Trillion in 2008," *Business Insider*, February 3, 2009, www.businessinsider.com/2009/2/america-lost-102-trillion -of-wealth-in-2008.

[6]John M. Goralka, "Estate Planning for an Aging Population," Wealth Management, July 5, 2016, www.wealthmanagement.com/estate-planning /estate-planning-aging-population.

11 Challenge to Generosity 2: A Desire for More

[1]Lucas Reilly, "By the Numbers: How Americans Spend Their Money," Mental Floss, July 17, 2012, www.mentalfloss.com/article/31222/numbers -how-americans-spend-their-money.

[2]Ibid.

[3]Ibid.

[4]Stephen Valdivia, Christina Austin, and Burcu Noyan, "The Scary Amount Americans Spend on Halloween," *Fortune*, October 27, 2015, www.fortune .com/video/2015/10/27/halloween-by-the-numbers-2015.

[5]Lou Carlozo, "Americans Will Spend $350 Million on Halloween Costumes. For Their Pets," *Christian Science Monitor*, October 14, 2015, www .csmonitor.com/Business/Saving-Money/2015/1014/Americans-will -spend-350-million-on-Halloween-costumes.-For-their-pets.

[6]"UK Golfers Spend £4bn Billion a Year Hallam Report Finds," Sheffield Hallam University, March 21, 2016, www4.shu.ac.uk/mediacentre/uk -golfers-spend-%C2%A34bn-year-hallam-report-finds.

[7]"Canadian Consumers Spending Big on Beauty: $1.4 Billion Dollar Beauty Market Ranks Canada Number One Globally," NPD Group, November 12, 2014, www.npdgroup.ca/wps/portal/npd/ca/news/press-releases/canadian -consumers-spending-big-on-beauty.

[8]Katya Kazakina, "Monet's Water Lilies Lead Sotheby's $20 Million Auction," Bloomberg, June 24, 2014, www.bloomberg.com/news/articles /2014-06-23/monet-s-water-lilies-sells-for-54-million-in-london.

[9]Hannah Parry, "Bright Pink Crocodile Skin Handbag Becomes the Most Expensive in the World After Selling for £150,000 in Hong Kong," *Daily*

Mail, June 1, 2015, www.dailymail.co.uk/news/article-3105801/Bright-pink
-crocodile-skin-handbag-expensive-world-selling-150-000-Hong-Kong.html.

[10]Scott Rafferty, "Floyd Mayweather Buys the Most Expensive Car in the World," *Rolling Stone,* August 24, 2015, www.rollingstone.com/sports/news/floyd-mayweather-buys-the-most-expensive-car-in-the-world-20150824.

[11]"Revenue of the Cosmetic Beauty Industry in the United States from 2002 to 2016 (in Billion U.S. Dollars)," *Statista,* www.statista.com/statistics/243742/revenue-of-the-cosmetic-industry-in-the-us.

[12]Curt Thompson, *The Soul of Shame: Retelling the Stories We Believe About Ourselves* (Downers Grove, IL: InterVarsity Press, 2015), 66.

[13]Daylle Deanna Schwartz, "Retail Therapy=Emotional Shopping," Lessons from a Recovering Doormat, Beliefnet, www.beliefnet.com/columnists/lessonsfromarecoveringdoormat/?s:retail+therapy.

[14]Chris Isidore, "Americans Spend More on the Lottery Than on . . ." CNN: Money, February 11, 2015, www.money.cnn.com/2015/02/11/news/companies/lottery-spending.

[15]Melissa Leong, "Why Do We Spend? What Science Says About Our Personal Finances," Financial Post, February 26, 2014, www.business.financialpost.com/personal-finance/why-do-we-spend-what-science-says-about-our-personal-finances.

[16]Ibid.

12 Challenge to Generosity 3: Subconscious Beliefs

[1]Renee Lockey, email to the author, February 17, 2017.

[2]But didn't Jesus say we would always have the poor with us? Yes, he did (Matthew 26:11). His statement, however, was directed to specific individuals who witnessed a specific event. When a woman poured expensive perfume on Jesus' feet shortly before his final days in Jerusalem, those who beheld the beautiful act criticized the lavishness of her gift because there were many poor people needing to be cared for. Jesus simply meant that those who were critical of her act of worship would always have the poor with them after he was gone. He was not making a prophetic statement for all time.

[3]"Global Poverty Is on the Decline, But Almost No One Believes It," Barna Group, April 28, 2014, www.barna.org/barna-update/culture/668-global-poverty-is-on-the-decline-but-almost-no-one-believes-it/.

[4]Ibid.

[5]Laurence Chandy, Hiroshi Kato, and Homi Kharas, "From a Billion to Zero: Three Key Ingredients to End Extreme Poverty," chap. 1 in *The Last Mile in Ending Extreme Poverty* (Washington, DC: Brookings institution Press, 2015), 5, www.brookings.edu/wp-content/uploads/2016/07 /Overview.pdf.

[6]*Poverty, Inc.*, historical documentary film, produced by James F. Fitzgerald, Jr., Michael Matheson Miller, 2014, www.povertyinc.org/about.

[7]Peter Debruge, "Film Review: 'Poverty Inc.,'" Variety, www.variety.com/2015 /film/reviews/poverty-inc-film-review-1201649597.

[8]"Lord's Resistance Army," The Enough Project, accessed May 20, 2016, www.enoughproject.org/conflicts/lra.

[9]Ann Montgomery, interview by the author, August 12, 2015.

13 Challenge to Generosity 4: Not Making a Plan

[1]Charles Duhigg, *The Power of Habit: Why We Do What We Do in Life and Business* (New York: Random House, 2014), 426, 503.

[2]Ibid., 112.

[3]Laura Arrillaga-Andreessen, *Giving 2.0: Transform Your Giving and Our World* (San Francisco: Jossey-Bass, 2012), 84.

[4]"Top 10 Worst Timing Ever," *Wrecked Exotics*, November 16, 2008, www .wreckedexotics.com/articles/016.shtml.

[5]Ibid.

15 Giving with Family

[1]Roy Williams and Vic Preisser, *Preparing Heirs: Five Steps to a Successful Transition of Family Wealth and Values* (San Francisco: Robert D. Reed Publishers, 2010), 3.

[2]Ibid., 48-49, 161.

[3]Ibid., 45.

[4]Ron Blue with Jeremy White, *Splitting Heirs: Giving Your Money and Things to Your Children Without Ruining Their Lives* (Chicago: Northfield Publishing, 2004), 45.

[5]Go to www.generousgiving.org/annual-celebrations.

[6]Go to www.generousgiving.org/small-gatherings.

[7]Randy Alcorn, *The Treasure Principle: Unlocking the Secret of Joyful Giving* (Colorado Springs: Multnomah Books, 2001).
[8]Jason Notte, "When is $5 Million Not Enough Personal Wealth?," *The Street*, June 1, 2015, www.thestreet.com/story/13177558/1/when-is-5-million -not-enough-personal-wealth.html.

16 Giving with Friends

[1]Sondra Shaw-Hardy and Martha A. Taylor, with Buffy Beaudoin-Schwartz, *Women and Philanthropy: Boldly Shaping a Better World* (San Francisco: Jossey-Bass, 2010), 148-49.
[2]Lacie Stevens and Patti Velasquez, eds., *God Calling: A Timeless Classic Updated in Today's Language* (Houston: Whitecaps Media, 2011).
[3]Scott Bader-Saye, *Following Jesus in a Culture of Fear (The Christian Practice of Everyday Life)* (Grand Rapids: Brazos Press, 2007), 69.

18 The (Unexpected?) Blessings of Giving

[1]"Global Christianity—A Report on the Size and Distribution of the World's Christian Population," Pew Research Center, December 19, 2011, www.pewforum.org/2011/12/19/global-christianity-exec.

INITIATIVES

Women Doing Well™ exists to ignite, resource, and connect women to live and give in God's image. Founded in 2010, Women Doing Well™ serves women by creating transformational experiences and tools designed to inspire and equip women to give more and more strategically of their wealth. In 2017, Women Doing Well™ became a ministry of **Generous Giving**. This partnership allowed each organization to better reach more women, their families, and communities with the life-changing message of generosity.

www.womendoingwell.org

www.generousgiving.org